COMMON
SENSE

COMMON SENSE

A PRIMER

THOMAS R. GILDERSLEEVE

iUniverse®

COMMON SENSE
A PRIMER

iUniverse books may be ordered through booksellers or by contacting:

iUniverse
1663 Liberty Drive
Bloomington, IN 47403
www.iuniverse.com
844-349-9409

ISBN: 978-1-6632-4686-8 (sc)
ISBN: 978-1-6632-4687-5 (e)

Print information available on the last page.

iUniverse rev. date: 11/08/2022

CONTENTS

We've been given life.
The question is: What do we do with it?

INTRODUCTION

There's nothing original in this book. Instead, it's a collection of the thought given to a variety of subjects. It's a primer of common sense.

CHAPTER ONE
Belief

All words have *connotation*. Connotation is what a word makes us think of.

When you hear the word dog, you may think of a large, longhaired animal. That's your connotation of the word dog.

I may think of a small, shorthaired animal. That's my connotation of the word dog.

The connotation that the word dog has for you is different from the connotation that the word has for me.

This is true in general. No two people have exactly the same connotation of a word.

However, various people's connotations of a word are similar enough to allow us to use the word in communication. Thus, you may think of a large animal when the word dog is mentioned, I may think of a small animal, Joe may think of a barking one, Pauline of one wagging its tail, and so on. But we all think of a four footed, hairy animal with a tail, snout, and prominent ears and can, consequently, talk about dogs.

In fact, if our connotations of a spoken group of sounds or a written group of letters weren't similar enough for us to use them in communicating with one another, they wouldn't be words. Words are sounds associated with groups of letters about which we've a large degree of agreement with respect to connotation. It's these common connotations that we find in the dictionary

Most words have *denotation*. Denotation is the relation that a word has to the thing it represents.

If we want to teach a child the denotation of the word dog, we may take him outside, walk around until we find a dog, point to the dog, and say the word, "Dog."

If the child understands what we're doing, he develops an idea of what a dog is. From this point on, the word dog has *meaning* for him. There's some connotation that comes to his mind when the word dog is mentioned. And he knows that, somewhere out in the world, there are things wandering around that bear some resemblance to his connotation of the word.

Not all denotation is exemplified by pointing. For example, no one has seen the Big Bang beginning of the universe. But the Big Bang is the explanation that best fits the available observations and mathematical calculations based on the equations that most reliably represent the world as we know it.

We humans are symbolic animals. We're forever inventing, using and modifying words.

We're unique in our use of symbols.

John's dog is a smart animal. He's so smart that he recognizes his master's name.

But when the dog hears the name John, his reaction is to start looking for his master. To the dog, the word John is a *signal* to indicate the presence of the word's denotation, just as a clap of thunder is a signal to us to start looking for rain.

In contrast to the dog, when we hear the word John, our reaction is to respond, "Yes, what about John?" That question is beyond the dog.

A word causes the dog to act with respect to the word's denotation. To the dog, the word is a signal.

A word causes us to act with respect to the word's connotation. An image is drawn up in our mind, and we prepare ourselves to receive more information with respect to this image. To us, the word is a *symbol*.

Our symbolic orientation is what allows us to formulate, store and communicate knowledge. However, it also lets us create symbols that have no denotation.

A harmless example of this behavior is the "purple people eater". The concept "purple people eater" draws up an image in our mind when it's mentioned. That is, the concept has connotation. Moreover, my connotation of a purple people eater is similar enough to yours to allow us to talk about purple people eaters.

The above situation is harmless because everybody realizes that the concept "purple people eater" has no denotation. There's nothing that you can point to and say, "There's a purple people eater." Nor is there anything that you can draw to people's attention and use as a basis for reasoning to the existence of purple people eaters.

As long as we create symbols having no denotation and recognize that they have no denotation, we're just amusing ourselves. However, if we create a symbol having no denotation but believe that it does, we're deluding ourselves.

We then believe in the existence of something that can be anything that we want it to be. When we act on the basis of such a belief, we can be led into error.

An example of this kind of behavior is the concept "witch". As Justice Louis Brandeis said, "Men feared witches and burnt women." (S 346)

So it becomes critical to be able to distinguish between symbols that have denotation and those that don't. The general procedure for doing this is to formulate a proposition about what the symbol stands for and then see if the proposition can be empirically verified.

For example, if the symbol is gravity, we can propose to drop a stone and see if it falls to the ground. Verifying that the stone did, indeed, fall to the ground doesn't guarantee that it always will in the future. But it lends credibility to the belief that the symbol, gravity, does have denotation.

We have more difficulty in determining whether some symbols have denotation than we do with others.

For example, witches are known for being able to make other people sick. There's an old woman who lives in a somewhat rundown house up the street. She has a black cat for a pet. She recently had a big argument with her next-door neighbor, and not two days after the argument, her neighbor came down with a chronic, disabling disease. Hmmm.

The data is often messy, which makes identifying words with no detonation difficult. We just have to do the best that we can.

However, there are several categories of discussion that are characterized by nonsense and delusion, because they deal with words that have no denotation.

One such category is aesthetics. It deals with beauty, a word without denotation.

You can identify things that you think are beautiful. But when it comes to talking about beauty in general, people don't know what they're talking about, because the word, beauty, has no objective referent. It's an abstract concept.

However, dealing in this nonsense is harmless. The worst that can happen is a heated argument over what is and isn't art, an argument that can never be resolved, because there's nothing objective on which to base a decision.

Another category of discussion where the use of words without denotation is characteristic is metaphysics. Metaphysics is concerned with the "reality" behind our sense perceptions, which rules out the possibility of denotation.

Just to be clear about it, metaphysics includes religion. In further explication, let me point out that, when the atheist denies the existence of God, he's dealing in the same nonobjective terms as is the believer.

When it comes to religion, the only tenable position is agnosticism. In contrast to the believer and the atheist, the agnostic maintains that all religious questions involve things about which it's impossible to know anything. So there's no point in even talking about them.

As Ludwig Wittgenstein has said, with respect to those things about which it's impossible to speak, one should remain silent. (Actually, his words were, in translation, of course, "Whereof one cannot speak, thereof one must be silent." (Wovon man nicht sprechen kann, daruber muss man schweigen, which is the final statement in Wittgenstein's seminal book, *Tractatus Logico-Philosophicus.* (K 220)))

When it comes to God, he/she/it/they can be anything that you want him/her/it/them to be, I can't prove that you're wrong, and you can't prove that you're right, so there's no point in discussing it.

Religion is a subject about which it's impossible to say anything definitive. And if you think that you can, you're deluding yourself.

From this perspective, religion is similar to aesthetics. It's just nonsense and isn't worth talking about.

But unlike aesthetics, religious delusion can be pernicious. Religious history has left a bloody trail, a process that continues into the present day.

And less catastrophic but still regrettable are the practices that religion imposes on people without a shred of evidence that the practices are of any value. Prohibiting efficient means of birth control and condemning women to an inferior role are examples.

Finally, objectively, ethics is out. It deals with right and wrong, words without denotation.

Sources

This material on connotation, denotation, signals and symbols comes from *Philosophy in a New Key* by Susanne K. Langer (Mentor 1951).

CHAPTER TWO
Ethics

Ethics has to do with right and wrong, words that have no denotation. We can point to instances of what we believe are right and wrong behavior. But there's no entity to which we can point and say, "Look, there's right." The same is equally true of right's opposite, wrong. Nor is there anything that you can draw to people's attention and use as a basis for reasoning to the presence of an entity constituting right or wrong.

Nevertheless, ethics is indispensable. Without it, we have no moral compass.

Because the words, right and wrong, have no denotation, an empirical approach is of no use in trying to develop ethics. Consequently, we have to find some other foundation on which to build our ethics.

Historically, religion has formed such a foundation. Despite this fact, religion seems to be a weak reed on which to rely for a guide to ethical behavior.

Never mind the apparently endless list of atrocities committed in the name of religion. Religion's claim to be the font of ethical knowledge is subject to even more serious question.

Religion deals with terms having no objective referent and appeals to revelation for its justification. There are books of revelations, such as the Torah, Bible and Quran. But the final arbiters of religious thought are the priests whose job it is to interpret the revelations.

So religious conclusions ultimately rest on authority, always a dangerous situation. Authority is good at enforcing already agreed on regulations. But it's not reliable when it comes to deciding what those regulations should be. It's partial to regulations that redound to the benefit of those in power rather than to the people in general.

Toward the end of the 18th century, a school of ethical thought called *utilitarianism* developed. Its most well-known architect was Jeremy Bentham.

The fundamental idea of utilitarianism is that what's ethical is that which results in the greatest happiness for the greatest number of people. Unfortunately, the calculus of figuring out what actions result in the greatest happiness for the greatest number of people is formidable. It's hardly a technique for making ethical choices on a moment-to-moment, personal basis.

And utilitarianism suffers from an even more grievous fault. Different people have differing concepts of what constitutes happiness, which in specific situations, can lead to different conclusions as to what the ethical thing to do is.

Who is it who's going to decide of what people's happiness consists? Once more, we're back to an appeal to authority. Maybe the way to promote the greatest happiness for the greatest number of people is to eliminate certain degenerate parts of the population. After all, that's what Hitler thought, and not everyone disagreed with him.

Relying on authority doesn't work when trying to come up with an ethical system. And consequently, utilitarianism doesn't cut it when it comes to serving as a basis for an ethic.

However, utilitarianism did make one contribution. It moved the discussion of ethics down from the cosmic struggle between God and the Devil to a concern with human beings and their condition, namely, their happiness.

Happiness is a difficult term to define. Given this difficulty, maybe we could focus on a similar, but somewhat less complicated, concept that we could accept as a proxy for happiness – pleasure.

Pleasure is also difficult to define. A start might be to recognize that we suffer pain and that the inability to satisfy our more basic drives, such as thirst and hunger, leads to discomfort and, ultimately, death. At a minimum, we could define pleasure as the avoidance of such pain, agony and disaster.

We can probably do even better than that. Satisfying drives, such as hunger and sex, seems to bring some kind of satisfaction that we could call pleasure.

The trouble is that, as we move away from the basic physiological drives and get into more self-actuated ones, such as enjoying music or sports, it becomes harder and harder to make general statements about pleasure. There's just too much variation from person to person.

But perhaps there's a way out. Since there's such variation in what people think of as pleasure, why not let each person decide for himself what gives him pleasure and then give him the right to act on the basis of his conclusions? In this way, we arrive at the idea that *freedom*, the right to act in whatever way a person sees fit, might form the foundation for an ethic.

If freedom gives us the right to act in whatever way that we see fit, then it should also give everyone else the same right. And this observation places restrictions on what we're free to do.

We can do anything that we want as long as we don't restrict the ability of anyone else to do what they want. This conclusion gives us an ethical principle that applies equally to all people, a rule that places your wishes on the same level as everyone else's: *As long as you avoid preventing anyone from doing what they want to do, you're free to do anything that you want.*

If we want to enjoy freedom, we have to constrain our actions to the extent that we avoid preventing anyone from doing what they want to do. This is an ethical responsibility. It's not right to prevent people from doing what they want to do, and we shouldn't do it.

As a further insight into the concept of freedom, consider the following series of steps, which are collectively known as the tale of the slave, a tale told by Robert Nozick in his book, *Anarchy, State, and Utopia.* As you read the tale of the slave, ask yourself: In what step or steps did you, the slave, experience an increase in freedom?

1. You're a slave. What meager possessions you have, a few rags for clothes and a place under a roof to sleep, you hold at your master's sufferance. The products of your efforts go to your master, who uses them as he sees fit. The activities in which your efforts are invested are selected by your master. Your master treats you

brutally. You're whipped and otherwise abused at his whim, are often underfed, and receive inadequate medical attention.

2. Your master acquires other slaves. Ultimately, he owns 10,000 slaves besides you. He treats his other slaves in the same way that he treats you.

3. Your master publishes a set of regulations concerning slave behavior. He whips or otherwise punishes a slave only if the slave violates a regulation.

4. Your master improves the living conditions of his slaves — supplies more ample clothing, improves the quality of the food, provides more adequate shelter, and arranges for medical services when required.

5. Your master decrees that his slaves will work for him only three days a week. The slaves can do whatever they want the other four days, but in return, the slaves must provide for their own needs — food, clothing, shelter, medical attention, etc.

6. Your master allows his slaves to leave the plantation and go wherever they want. He requires only that each slave leaving the plantation send back to the plantation, each week, three sevenths of the slave's income. The rest the slave may keep to do with as he wishes. Your master retains the power to raise, lower or change the form of the levy on slave income. He also retains the power to recall the slaves to the plantation in case of what he sees as an emergency.

7. Your master turns ownership of the plantation over to the 10,000 other slaves as a group. Of all the slaves, only you aren't included in this ownership transfer. The 10,000 slaves now vote on how the plantation is to be run and what the duties of the slaves to the plantation are. Majority rules on all matters.

8. If the other slaves are deadlocked on a question, 5000 for and 5000 against, they let you determine the issue.

9. The other slaves decide to treat you just like one of them. Your vote on plantation issues is now mingled with the other 10,000.

Freedom is the right to choose. So your only increase in freedom came in step five, when you were allowed to have four days a week to yourself. However, even then, you were still, to a considerable extent, a slave.

In step seven, you turned in a one headed master for a 10,000 headed one. But your slave status hadn't changed since step five. Even in step nine, where we have adherence to the principle of one-person/one-vote, your control over your actions is small, as is made clear in step eight.

Your freedom is restricted to the extent to which you can be forced to do something that you'd otherwise choose to not do. So, a precondition for freedom is the absence of *force*.

The requirement to not use force against other people is an ethical responsibility. The power of an ethical responsibility should never be underestimated.

However, as Saint Paul said, the spirit may be willing, but the flesh is sometimes weak. Given the natural proclivities of humans for gratification and the accumulation of wealth and power, it's not surprising that some exploit others despite the ethical prohibition against doing so.

It's disheartening to realize that, if someone is determined to force you to do something that you don't want to do, the only alternative to submission is to resist, which at the least, involves the threat of retaliation. The promised retaliation doesn't have to be direct. The classic case is, "You do that, and my big brother will get you."

Consequently, freedom is a state that we can approach but can't completely reach. A policy of freedom must be to minimize, rather than eliminate, force.

The way that a society minimizes force is to become a political body with a government, which is given the exclusive right to use force. Only the government has police power.

The government has police power to prevent the use of force by one private entity on another. Thus, the government becomes "big brother", to whom recourse is made when you're threatened with or are subject to violence.

The government's exclusive right to use force presents the danger that those persons representing the government may seize the government's police power to force their will on us. One protection against such power seizure is limitation of the government's ability to use force to those instances where general rules, previously set up, allow for this use. These rules, that describe the limits of the government's police power, are *laws*.

Laws are general. They're worded with respect to everybody and refer to general acts.

Laws don't say that only redheads must replace the property that they've destroyed. Either everybody must make restitution or nobody has to.

Laws don't say that hitting someone with a baseball bat is assault. They say that inflicting bodily harm is assault regardless of method.

A society in which the extent of the government's police power is limited by laws is living under *the rule of law*. Under the rule of law, you know that you'll never become subject to the government's police power as long as you conform to the law, knowledge of which is available to you before you act.

The opposite of the rule of law is the rule of people. Under the rule of people, your every action is dependent on the government's arbitrary approval. Under the rule of law, the government's only purpose is to decide whether your action conforms to the law.

Under the rule of people, government is represented by the king, dictator or administrator. Under the rule of law, government is represented by the judge.

Since law is by nature general, it can never cover particulars. Therefore, law always has to be interpreted.

The interpretation is made by a judge. And the interpretation made of law varies with the judge making the interpretation.

Consequently, it has been maintained that there's no such thing as a rule of law. There's only the rule of people.

Nevertheless, the difference between the force imposed on you by the interpretations of a judge, who must heed both the wording of the law and the precedents established by previous rulings on the law, and the power over your action wielded by an administrator, who need appeal only to the power vested in him, marks the distinction between the rule of law and the rule of people.

We introduced the rule of law into the tale of the slave in step three, when your master set down the regulations, breach of which alone results in punishment. If your actions stay within the regulations, you don't have to fear punishment. But you're still a slave and have to do what your master says.

The rule of law eliminates capricious punishment. But it doesn't create freedom.

As exemplified in step three of the tale of the slave, a person can live under the rule of law and still be a complete slave. Your every action is still at the beck and call of your master. The rule of law and slavery aren't incompatible.

Given that a society becomes a political body with a government invested with the responsibility for preventing the use of force by one person on another, the question arises as to which persons in the society are to carry out this responsibility. One answer to this question is democracy, in which the members of the society choose their government by voting.

Democracy has a lot to recommend it. It provides for an orderly transition and resultant continuity of government. And it gives citizens the feeling that they can participate in the choice of their government, which contributes to political stability. As has been truly said, democracy may not look attractive ... until you consider the alternatives.

But of all the things that democracy is, the thing that it's often touted for is the thing that it's not. Democracy is persistently presented as equivalent to freedom. This is wrong.

There's no connection between freedom and democracy. A society can be democratic and elect to become a tyranny.

To choose one's government isn't to have freedom. This fact is demonstrated in step nine of the tale of the slave, where a one-person/one-vote democracy has been established, but where freedom hasn't increased since your single master gave you the choice of what you wanted to do four days out of seven back in step five.

So, democracy under the rule of law doesn't guarantee freedom. A pure democracy subjects the minority to the will of the majority, as exemplified in step seven of the tale of the slave, when you turned in a one-headed master for a 10,000 headed one with no increase in freedom.

Limited government is necessary to freedom. Under a limited government, citizens have rights that can't be taken away by government action. In the US, these rights are spelled out in our Constitution.

To see that our rights are protected, the Supreme Court decides what legislation and actions are constitutional or unconstitutional, and the executive branch enforces the Court's decisions. This is, pretty much, a jury rig, and it doesn't always work.

But amazingly, in the main, it does work. And it does because we believe in it. As Judge Learned Hand said:

> I often wonder whether we do not rest our hopes too much
> upon constitutions, upon laws, and upon courts. These
> are false hopes; believe me, these are false hopes. Liberty
> lies in the hearts of men and women; when it dies there,
> no constitution, no law, no court can save it.

To be free is to have the ability to choose among actions. With freedom comes the responsibility to live with the results of our actions.

Freedom to act is the freedom to take chances and make mistakes. Regardless of the discomfort that such mistakes cause, if we want freedom, we must accept the responsibility for our mistakes and deal with the consequences ourselves.

We do have to be cognizant of diminished capacity. Lesions in the brain can reduce a person's capacity to control his actions. Psychological problems can reduce a person's ability to recognize situations for what they are. And it may be that these psychological problems are based on a chemical imbalance in the brain.

The ability to hold people responsible for their actions has to be mitigated in the face of diminished capacity. Nevertheless, in general, people are responsible for their actions.

If an increase in freedom is good, and a decrease, bad, then ethically, our approach to behavior should be to reduce force to the minimum possible. Any action on the part of anyone to restrict the freedom of another increases the exploitation in the situation.

With every increase in the use of force, the lowering of the general welfare toward Hobbes' state of nature increases. Even if, in a particular situation, we can't foresee the ill effects of a restriction of freedom, the ill effects will, nevertheless, occur. Our failure to anticipate the undesirable consequences is no argument for instituting the restriction.

One way to decide if something is *ethical* is to ask, "Is force being used to restrict anyone's freedom of action?" If not, then nothing unethical is going on.

For example, the government currently spends a lot of time, effort and money prosecuting the production, distribution and use of drugs. But clearly, producing, distributing and using drugs aren't unethical. No one forces the drug user to use drugs. And producing and selling drugs is no different from producing and selling any other kind of product.

Not only does prosecuting the drug business waste tax dollars, contribute to a burgeoning prison population, undermine the governments of countries where drugs are grown, and finance terrorists, criminalizing this activity results in the creation of extralegal organizations that service the demand for drugs.

The objection to extralegal organizations isn't that they provide goods to meet a demand. What's offensive about these extralegal organizations is the inevitable violence with which they conduct their business. They're, by definition, extralegal and, thus, have no access to courts for the redress of grievances.

Extralegal organizations aren't only suppliers. They're also enforcers.

These organizations are enforcers because, unlike legal organizations, they're unable to turn to the police and court system for enforcement of their rights. They have to do it themselves. Decriminalization of the products of these extralegal organizations would eliminate the need for their private enforcement activities.

Drug addiction is a problem, which can be approached in two possible ways. We can criminalize the production, distribution and use of drugs, which is the approach that we've adopted so far, and it hasn't worked very well. Or we could treat drug addiction as an illness, provide programs to both treat and prevent addiction, legalize the production, distribution and use of drugs, get the benefit of taxation on the sale of drugs, and avoid all of the ills that criminalization creates.

How about prostitution? If there's no extortion involved, prostitution doesn't force anybody to do anything. Voluntary prostitutes should have the unrestricted right to carry on their trade.

Pornography takes on the aspect of a perversion. But again, absent extortion, no one is being forced to do anything. Instead of suppressing pornography, an educational program related to its ill effects might be more productive.

It's with respect to the question of what our attitude should be toward the use of such things as tobacco, alcohol, drugs and pornography that the distinction between adults and children comes into play. While we've come to the conclusion that a person who has reached his maturity should be free to choose his actions and take the responsibility for them, we have reason to worry about the judgment of children when it comes to use of what could be damaging products, because their immature brains aren't yet ready to responsibly make decisions of such gravity.

It would be nice if we could just leave it up to parents to see that their children don't misuse these goods, but the fact is that children tend to be influenced by their peers at least as much as they are by their parents. As a consequence, it makes sense to have society place restraints on the availability of these products for the use of children.

Is the minimum wage ethical? It forces employers to pay their employees more than they voluntarily choose to do.

The fundamental problem here is that some people don't earn enough to support themselves. Employers may respond to a minimum wage by moving their operation to where labor is less expensive, raising their prices, eliminating positions, or shutting down, none of which is good for people who already aren't earning enough to support themselves. A better alternative would be to expand the earned income tax credit.

Is forcing employers to provide health care coverage for their employees ethical? Doubtful, and it just complicates an already difficult health care problem, which we'll take up in the chapter on government.

Is affirmative action ethical? Again, doubtful, and it just forces employers and institutions to accept people other than those whom they would otherwise chose.

The question here is who gets to do what in society — for example, who gets to join the society's universities, professions, and public offices? Each such entity has the mission of producing a certain good, and this mission should determine who are selected.

For example, the mission of a symphony orchestra is to produce great music, and that means that the people selected for membership in the orchestra should be those who are the most gifted musically. Commercial plane flights should be under the command of the best pilots. Surgery should be performed by the best surgeons. To select otherwise would be to reduce the ability to realize the given mission. (S 178,179,186) And in assigning jobs on the basis of merit, there's no justification for considering irrelevant factors such as race.

Whether you're free doesn't depend on the choices open to you in the circumstances in which you find yourself. You may not have the natural ability to be a basketball star no matter how much you desire to and work hard and diligently to become one. You may not have the smarts to earn the income that you'd like to enjoy.

There are all kinds of circumstances that limit choice. But that doesn't make you a slave. You're a slave when someone can force you to do what they want you to do whether or not you want to do it.

Slavery is a function of force, not a function of circumstances. It depends on whether you can act according to your wishes or are subject to another's interests. That a person is caught in circumstances where he has to work at an unsatisfying job that hardly pays enough to provide for life's necessities is regrettable and calls for action to avoid such situations, but it isn't slavery.

Freedom, where you can do anything that you want as long as you don't prevent anyone from doing what they want, sounds like a pretty good idea. And it is.

Freedom has a lot to recommend it. Freedom allows each of us to enjoy life in the way that we deem fit. It stimulates the exchange of ideas, which leads to invention, innovation, and increased productivity. But it isn't without problems.

Freedom prohibits John from selling Tom into slavery because John would be forcing Tom into a situation where he would no longer be in control of what he wants to do. Instead, he would be forced to do whatever his master wants.

But what if Tom wants to sell himself into slavery? If he can find a buyer, Tom isn't exercising force against anyone.

There's no ethical reason for preventing Tom from carrying out the sale. And if Tom wants John to act as Tom's agent and even make a profit from the sale, and if John is willing, once more, no force is being exercised, and freedom has no objection to the sale.

However, we find slavery abhorrent. (S ch 3) That's why we arbitrarily define our property rights in ourselves (our thoughts, will and action) as inalienable rights, rights not available for transfer, by sale or gift. So, what we have here is a case where we choose to give a value, the inalienability of our freedom, precedence over the dictates of freedom.

You have freedom when you can choose your actions to satisfy your wishes whether they conform to anyone else's wishes or not. What a person does with his freedom has no bearing on his right to his freedom. Not only is he free to live in a way repugnant to you, work when you traditionally rest, and find his interests in activities that you consider vulgar, he's also free to place his life in jeopardy, be prodigal when he's young and suffer in his old age, abuse himself, act so as to make himself destitute, and starve. Warn him you can, exhort him you may, help him you can try, but force him you may not.

Freedom allows those who desire to be charitable to give no end of materials, time and effort to any cause that they wish. It only denies them the right to militate against those who refuse these gifts or decline to participate in the giving.

Suppose that John has made no provisions for his old age. When he becomes so old that he's no longer able to support himself, should we let him die in the street?

From the point of view of freedom, the answer is clear. Yes, we should.

No one is responsible for John but John. He's the one who chose not to provide for himself. Consequently, he should suffer the consequences.

But are we willing to abide by our convictions in this area? Many of us aren't. Many give to charity to help out those in need.

And that's OK. Charity is a voluntary activity. No one is forcing anyone to do anything.

But charity typically lacks the resources to completely do the job. What then? Apparently, the majority of us feel that the government should step in.

The high-minded argument goes like this. Everyone has the right to live out his life with at least a minimum of dignity. And it's up to the government to see that this right is respected. The reality may be that we just can't stomach the idea of stepping over dead and dying bodies lying on the sidewalk.

In any case, our government has set up a program to see that everyone has some minimum amount of retirement income. That costs money. From where is this money to come?

It shouldn't come from the government's general revenue. That would force people, who don't want to, to contribute to John's welfare.

It's John's welfare about which we're talking here. So he's the one who should pay for it. The government's program forces John to provide for his own retirement even if he doesn't want to.

To suave our conscience about forcing John to do what he may not want to do, the government's program is set up so everyone has to contribute to providing for their retirement in the same way John has to. The program is designed to be nondiscriminatory and, thus, considered to be acceptable.

All in all, it's not a bad program. We're just forcing people to do what they should be doing anyhow.

Nevertheless, we should always keep in mind that compelling people to do things isn't generally a good idea.

If service providers, such as bakers and photographers, don't want to make their services available to certain parties, is it ethical to force them to do so? Freedom says no.

If owners of places of public accommodation want to choose those whom they're willing to accommodate, should they be forced to accommodate everyone without exception? Again, freedom says no.

Should people be able to pass zoning ordinances to govern property use in their community? Probably, although we're now getting close to the exercise of tyranny by the majority over the minority.

But systematic adherence to the right to restrict property use by one group with respect to another group could result in freezing the second group out of much of public life, which goes against our commitment to equality of opportunity.

So, we come to the conclusion that if hotels, restaurants, and, yes, bakers and photographers, are places that offer their services to the public, then they must be open to all and serve the public without discrimination.

Freedom has nothing to do with wealth. Whether you're free and whether you're rich are different questions.

Lack of money may be a condition that limits your choice, but it doesn't reduce your freedom. The only time that your freedom is reduced is when someone uses force on you to compel you to do other than what you'd have done had the force not been applied.

Of course, the options open to a person in extreme economic privation are limited, and we question the extent to which we should allow such conditions to exist. We also wonder about the extent to which the person is responsible for his condition. We wrestle with these challenges to our warring values in the attempt to determine what the right thing to do is.

Then, there's the question of campaign contributions. From the perspective of freedom, a person or organization ought to be able to contribute just as much as they want to a politician's campaign.

But we prohibit the bribing of politicians, because it debases government. And to what extent is a campaign contribution different from a bribe?

Sometimes it's neither freedom nor values that determine things. Instead, hard facts take precedence.

Abortion is an example. Killing a person is murder, and that's what abortion is. If that was all that there was to it, deciding what position to take with respect to abortion would be a straightforward matter. However:

An abortion is the result of an unwanted pregnancy. And whether an unwanted pregnancy brought to term creates a situation that's worse than an abortion is an open question.

The hard fact is that women who want an abortion are going to get one whether it's legal or not. In fact, the number of abortions performed in countries where it's illegal is greater than the number performed in countries where it's legal (P 343). And legal abortions are safer than illegal ones.

So maybe it's better to legalize abortion. But doing so shouldn't cause us to look on the act as anything other than unethical, repugnant, and something to be avoided if at all possible, which ought to be most of the time. After all, this is the age of birth control.

Our investigation into freedom has demonstrated that, while it may be a good guide to follow, it isn't universally applicable. We have values that take precedence over freedom. People shouldn't be allowed to sell themselves into slavery. People should have equal opportunity to pursue happiness. People shouldn't have to suffer the extreme consequences of not providing for their retirement. Things should be fair. Rich people and organizations shouldn't be allowed to corrupt the political process. Etc.

We can't live without value-laden attitudes as to what commitments we have to family, community and nation. It's those attitudes that define what we are and that bind us together.

But we have to be careful about this kind of thinking. Every atrocity that Soviet Russia committed against its people was justified on the basis of the argument that it was in their interests. All societies are value laden and some of them, such as those endorsing Nazism and Communism, go too far in violating individual rights and, consequently, aren't following ethically acceptable practices.

When it comes to values, perhaps the best that we can do is adopt those that, over time, have proved beneficial and avoid those that don't work out well. For example: Beware of idealists. Beware of paternalism. Be fair. Be honest. Do justice. Love mercy. Have compassion. Be humble. Be kind. Be considerate. Be tolerant. Be responsible. Revere family, community and country.

Here I'm just exposing you to my prejudices. Other people would have a different lists of values, some of which might be incompatible with mine.

And we shouldn't overlook the fact that some of our own values may be incompatible. For example, being merciful is incompatible with doing justice. And when does kindness degenerate into paternalism? Here we have to establish priorities, which is also a value judgment.

One of the most fundamental value judgments that our experience has taught us to make is to respect freedom. It's a kind of sheet anchor to keep our actions from going too far off course.

Sources

(H) Hayek *The Constitution of Liberty*
(N) Nozick, Robert *Anarchy, State, and Utopia*
(P) Pasternak, Charles *Quest* (Wiley 2003)
(S) Sandel, Michael J. *Justice* (Farrar, Straus and Giroux 2009)

CHAPTER THREE

Knowledge

If we're at point A and want to be at point B, we know that we can get to point B in a number of ways – we can walk, bicycle, drive, take a taxi, or hop a subway, bus, train or plane. The method that we choose depends on a number of factors – how far point B is from point A, what forms of transportation are available, what the schedules are, what our finances are, and so on.

We also know that there are a lot of other actions, such as talking, sleeping or eating, that won't get us to point B. To get to point B, we have to choose one of those few actions, out of the many available, that will get us to point B.

If we're in the living room and want to be in the kitchen, we know that, if we face the kitchen and keep putting one foot in front of the other, we'll end up in the kitchen.

What is this that we know? What is this *knowledge* that we have that walking transports us, that drinking relieves thirst, that water runs downhill, that dropped objects fall to the ground, and so on?

Knowledge is the memory of experience, both ours and other people's. For example, if every time that we drop an object, it falls to the ground, and if everyone whom we meet tells us that, every time they drop an object, it falls to the ground, we conclude that dropped objects always fall to the ground.

Then we know that, if we have a stone in our hand, we can safely let it go, because it will only drop harmlessly to the ground. It won't fly up and hit us in the face, explode, or float freely in the air.

Knowledge always has this form.

Dropped objects have always fallen to the ground in the past. Therefore, they'll always fall to the ground in the future.

Water has always run downhill in the past. Therefore, it will always run downhill in the future.

Something has always happened in a particular way in the past. Therefore, it will always happen in that same way in the future.

In general:

> In the past, X has always been the case. Therefore, X will always be the case in the future.

This way of coming to a general conclusion by reasoning from a large number of particular instances is known as *induction*.

To repeat, knowledge always has the following form.

> In the past, X has always been the case. Therefore, X will always be the case in the future.

My question is: What makes you think so? The fact that water has always run downhill in the past doesn't exclude the possibility that, the next time that you look at a stream, it may be running uphill. And the fact that every stone dropped in the past has fallen to the ground doesn't exclude the possibility that, the next time that you drop a stone, it may start rising in the air."

By now you're probably pretty exasperated, and you may exclaim something like, "For Pete's sake! I've always expected something that has always happened in a certain way in the past to happen the same way in the future, and I've always been right."

From a pragmatic point of view, this may be the proper attitude. But as a logical argument, it just won't hold.

Look at what you're saying. Once more, the form that knowledge takes is:

In the past, X has always been the case. Therefore, X will always be the case in the future.

Suppose that we let the X in this knowledge form be the statement, "What has happened in a certain way in the past always happens the same way in the future." Then what you're saying is that this specific X has always been the case in the past, and you're trying to persuade me that, therefore, it will always be the case in the future.

But in so doing, you're using the proposition that you're trying to prove. That's not logically permissible.

There's no way out. The fact that something has always been the case in the past can't guarantee that it will always be the case in the future. It may be a useful heuristic, but it can't make claim to unassailable truth.

Guiding our behavior on the basis of inductive knowledge is an act of faith. We can't prove that using inductive knowledge to guide behavior is the surest way to achieve our goals. Our decision to do so is an act of faith, a commitment to a principle on which we're willing to hazard our welfare.

The reason that we make this commitment is pragmatic. Use of inductive knowledge to guide our behavior seems to work in that it tends to produce the results that we want.

The body of propositions that we call knowledge isn't constant. What we believed to be the case yesterday isn't necessarily what we believe to be the case today, and what we believe today may not be what we'll believe tomorrow.

We once believed that the world was the center of the universe and that it was flat. As a consequence, we were led into error — that is, actions based on these beliefs didn't get us where we wanted to go. So we refined these beliefs to reconcile them with the new facts that our errors uncovered.

This process continues today. Knowledge isn't an absolute.

Knowledge is a body of beliefs that's the most useful that we can assemble at the moment. Tomorrow we'll be able to refine it further. As we act on our beliefs and make mistakes, we clarify our knowledge to make it progressively more useful in pursuing our goals.

The branch of philosophy with which we've been concerned here is *epistemology*, and today, most epistemologists would agree that the way to knowledge is by induction.

Sources

The epistemological theory presented here is known as *logical positivism*. Logical positivism was developed by the Vienna Circle, which stood in admiration of Wittgenstein and his book *Tractatus Logico-Philosophicus*, and although a contemporary of the Circle, Wittgenstein was never a part of it.

A. J. Ayer, an English philosopher, traveled to Vienna to study with the Circle, and on his return to England, he wrote his book, *Language, Truth and Logic*, which is considered to be the most explicit statement of logical positivism in English.

CHAPTER FOUR

Logic

Logic is reasoning from premises to conclusions. Mathematics is a subset of logic.

Unlike the symbols that are used in knowledge, which have denotation, the symbols used in logic have no denotation.

There's no place that I can take you and show you a one or a seven. I can show you one bowling ball or one flower pot or one what-have-you, but I can't show you anything that the concept, one, represents, because one, like all numbers, is an ideal concept and has no denotation.

Nor is there any place that I can take you and show you a straight line. I can show you approximations of a straight line, but the straight line, per se, is an ideal concept and has no denotation.

The same thing is true of a point. I can show you approximations of a point, but the mathematical symbol, point, is an ideal concept. For example, it has no dimension, something impossible in the real world.

Yet we rely on logic, because unlike knowledge, which is just probable, logic is certain. Two plus two is four, now and forever. There's no question about it. Logic isn't like knowledge, where conclusions are subject to question and qualification.

Logic is certain because it consists of *tautologies*. It's nothing but *deductions* made from a set of definitions called *axioms*.

For example, Euclidean geometry has a small number of axioms, and from these axioms are deduced a large number of theorems. We're astounded when we discover some of the theorems that come out of this process.

But the theorems are all implicit in the definitions of the axioms. If we were smart enough, we'd immediately see all of the tautological theorems residing in the axioms, and Euclidean geometry would be dull stuff.

It's its tautological character that makes logic unquestionably true. You can't deny that A is A.

There's just one flaw in the claim of logic to certainty. Deduction has to start somewhere, so back at the beginning, you have to accept, as premises, a small number of axioms.

Such a necessity gives one pause, because suppose that, against all odds, one of your axioms turns out to be false. In such a case, all is lost. Logicians try to protect against such a possibility by keeping their axioms to a minimum and confining them to assumptions that don't lead to contradictions.

Mathematics comes into use in science when its axioms approximate a situation in the real world closely enough to be able to use the deductions from the axioms in furthering the scientific investigation.

For example, for small plots of land on the Earth's surface, the Euclidean axioms closely approximate the real situation, and Euclidean theorems can be used to determine certain facts in the situation. Thus, by determining the angle at which the sun is striking a tree and measuring the length of its shadow, you can figure out how tall the tree is.

But for large surfaces of the Earth, Euclidean geometry won't do, for the Earth isn't flat, it's spherical, and to deal with this situation, a different kind of geometry, one with different axioms than those of Euclidean geometry, is necessary.

When used in science, mathematical equations represent relationships. Symbols are assigned to physical concepts such as mass and electrical current. These symbols are combined in equations to represent the physical relationships involving these concepts.

One of the interesting aspects of this use of mathematics to describe physical situations is that subsequent manipulations of the equations set up to represent recognized physical relationships can predict other phenomena that have previously escaped recognition but that, on investigation, prove to be the case. (S) For example, when James Clerk Maxwell put together his equations describing electromagnetics, one of the facts that dropped out was that the speed of light was a constant.

Logic consists of *valid arguments*.

Here's an example of an argument.

> If A, then B.
> A.
> Therefore, B.

This argument is made up of three *propositions*: "If A, then B", "A", and "Therefore, B". The first two propositions ("If A, then B" and "A") are *premises*. The third proposition ("Therefore, B") is a *conclusion*.

The first proposition is a *conditional*. The phrase following the "If" in the conditional is the *antecedent*. The phrase following the "then" is the *consequent*. In the conditional "If A, then B", "A" is the antecedent and "B" the consequent.

If the conclusion of an argument follows from the premises, then the argument is *valid*. If the premises of a valid argument are *true*, then the conclusion is true.

One class of arguments is conditional arguments, arguments in which one or more of the premises is a conditional. The example argument given above is a conditional argument.

Here are characteristic conditional arguments, both valid and invalid.

Asserting the Antecedent (B 53,54)

The argument:

> If A, then B.
> A.
> Therefore, B.

is called *asserting the antecedent*, and it's a valid argument, which can be proven as follows.

There are four possible combinations of the antecedent and the consequent.

1. A and B.
2. A and not-B.
3. Not-A and B.
4. Not-A and not-B.

The proposition "If A, then B" eliminates possibility 2 – if "A" is the case, then it can't be that "B" isn't the case. The proposition, "A" eliminates possibilities 3 and 4 – if "A" is the case, then it can't be that "A" isn't the case.

That leaves possibility 1 as the only remaining possibility, and it says that, when we have "A", then we have "B". Therefore, asserting the antecedent is a valid argument.

Here's an example of asserting the antecedent.

> If they play Handel (A), then I'll enjoy the program (B).
> They're going to play Handel (A).
> Therefore, I'll enjoy the program (B).

Asserting the Consequent (B 55-58)

The form of the argument of asserting the consequent is a follows.

> If A, then B.
> B.
> Therefore, A.

We analyze this argument as follows. As we've already determined, there are four possible combinations of "A" and "B".

1. A and B.
2. A and not-B.
3. Not-A and B.
4. Not-A and not-B.

And as usual, the proposition, "If A, then B", eliminates possibility 2. The proposition "B" eliminates possibilities 2 and 4.

Possibilities 1 and 3 remain, and possibility 3 says that we can have both "B" and "not-A". So asserting the consequent isn't a valid argument.

To return to our concert going example, that I enjoyed the concert (B), doesn't mean that Handel was on the program (A). Perhaps it was Vivaldi, rather than Handel, who was on the program and I enjoy Vivaldi as much as I enjoy Handel.

Denying the Consequent (B 59)

The form of the argument is a follows.

> If A, then B.
> Not B.
> Therefore, not-A.

There are four possible combinations of "A" and "B".

1. A and B.
2. A and not-B.
3. Not-A and B.
4. Not-A and not-B.

The proposition, "If A, then B", eliminates possibility 2. The proposition "not-B" eliminates possibilities 1 and 3, which leaves us with possibility 4, which says that when we have "not-B" we also have "not-A". So *denying the consequent* is valid. That I didn't enjoy the concert (not B) guarantees that Handel wasn't on the program (not-A).

Denying the Antecedent (B 58)

The form of the argument is:

> If A, then B.
> Not A.
> Therefore, not-B.

The proposition, "If A, then B", eliminates possibility 2. The proposition "not-A" eliminates possibilities 1 and 2.

Propositions 3 and 4 remain as possibilities, and possibility 3 says that we can have both "not-A" and "B". Denying the antecedent isn't valid.

That Handel wasn't on the program (not-A) doesn't mean that I didn't enjoy the concert (not-B). I enjoy lots of other composers as much as I enjoy Handel.

Chain Argument (B 77,78)

The argument is:

> If A, then B.
> If B, then C.
> Therefore, if A, then C.

There are now eight possibilities.

1. A, B and C.
2. A, B and not-C.
3. A, not-B and C.
4. A, not-B and not-C.
5. Not-A, B and C.
6. Not-A, B and not-C.
7. Not-A, not-B and C.
8. Not-A, not-B and not-C.

Possibilities 2 and 4 are the only possibilities where we can have "A" and "not-C". The proposition, "If A, then B", eliminates possibility 4. The proposition, "If B, then C", eliminates possibility 2.

So it must be the case that, when we have A, we must also have C. The *chain argument* is valid.

> If they play Handel (A), then I'll enjoy the program (B).
> If I'll enjoy the program (B), then I'll go to the concert (C).
> Therefore, if they play Handel (A), then I'll go to the concert (C).

Indirect Argument (B 81)

> The argument is:

> If P, then not-P.
> Therefore, not-P.

The proposition, "If P, then not-P", eliminates the possibility of "P". So, what we have left is "not-P". The *indirect argument* is valid.

For example, consider the proposition, "Every rule has an exception" (P). This proposition is, itself, a rule.

So, according to the rule that every rule has an exception, this rule, that every rule has an exception, must, itself, have an exception. Which means that there must be a rule that doesn't have an exception (not-P). Therefore, it isn't the case that every rule has an exception (not-P).

Reductio ad Absurdum (B 82,83)

> The argument is:

> If not-A, then B.
> If not-A, then not-B.
> Therefore, A.

The proposition, "If not-A, then B", eliminates the possibility of "not-A" and "not-B". The proposition, "If not-A, then not-B", eliminates the possibility of "not-A and B". That leaves the possibility of "A and B" and the possibility of "A and not-B".

So, regardless of whether or not we have "B", we always have "A". *Reductio ad absurdum* is a valid argument.

For example, suppose that we want to prove that the square root of 2 isn't a rational number (A). We adopt the proposition that the square root of 2 is a rational number (not-A). Then there must be two integers, i and j, such that i/j is equal to the square root of 2.

To eliminate any factors that i and j might share, we divide both i and j by these common factors until we arrive at a fraction, m/n, where m and n have no common factors (B). That gives;

(1) $2^{1/2}$ = m/n

Squaring both sides of equation (1) gives:

(2) $2 = m^2/n^2$

which can be rearranged as follows:

(3) $2n^2 = m^2$

$2n^2$ is an even number. Therefore, m^2 must be an even number. As a consequence, m must also be an even number — that is, it must be equal to 2 times some other number, p.

(4) m = 2p

Substituting from equation (4) into equation (3) gives:

(5) $2n^2 = (2p)^2 = 4p^2$

which reduces to:

(6) $n^2 = 2p^2$

which means that n^2 is an even number, and that means that n is also an even number.

So, both m and n are even numbers. So they have a common factor (not-B), namely, two.

Consequently, the square root of 2 isn't a rational number (A).

Sources

(B) Black, Max *Critical Thinking* (Prentice-Hall 1946)
(S) Soros, George *In Defense of Open Society* (Hachette 2019)

CHAPTER FIVE

Instinct

Up to now in this book, we've concentrated on things such as ethics, science, logic and mathematics, things that our rational mind uses to decide what action to take. But our rational mind isn't the only factor involved in decision making. Over our evolutionary history, certain *instincts* have been built into our psyche.

This process has been going on for 500 million years and is what has allowed us and our vertebrae forbearers to survive and evolve. (In contrast, the rational mind is only 200,000 years old.)

Over time, our instincts have evolved into an exquisite decision making machine (L 17,24,25,100 K 11). They operate automatically and are extremely rapid, giving you answers almost instantaneously, which is just what you want if you live in a world where the possibility of being treated as prey is ever present, a situation that has pertained for a large part of our history and for all of the long history of those creatures that came before us.

Often our instincts lead to good decisions, but it pays to be aware of them, because they can lead us into error.

For example, to some extent, you determine the distance that an object is from you by how large the object appears. This tendency has some validity, since the further an object is from you, the smaller it appears.

But this tendency can get you into trouble. For example, when you look into your right rear-vision mirror, the car behind you on your right looks small, which leads you to believe that it's a long way away, when in fact, it's right on top of you.

We've a built-in set of fears, such as of spiders, snakes, enclosed spaces, and male strangers, developed by our forbearers to warn them to approach dangerous situations with caution. (Ka). The reason why what we consider to be "bad" foods (fat, salt and sugar) are so tasty is because they're high in energy and, in our ancestors' time, in short supply, so our forefathers developed a taste for them.

Our instincts operate automatically and are always turned on. Unless you consciously engage your rational mind, your instincts will automatically make your decisions for you. (K 28)

Here are some of our instincts.

Loss Aversion

We avoid large losses. This is a good idea, but it can lead us into making mistakes.

We come by our aversion to loss for good evolutionary reasons. Our ancestors were programmed to look for opportunities to eat and have sex, because these activities contributed to the survival of the species.

But trumping both of these proclivities was the urge to avoid harm, which could be fatal and, consequently, wouldn't be good for the preservation of the species. As a result, evolution encouraged us to shy away from even the threat of harm. There would always be time for food and sex another day. We're averse to loss by nature.

Suppose that you're given the choice between two options. You can choose between receiving $850,000 for certain or taking a gamble where there's a 90 percent chance of winning a million dollars and a ten percent chance of not getting anything at all.

The second option is uncertain, and statistics gives us a rational method for valuing it. The method is called *expected value*, and it goes like this.

The expected value of a proposition is the sum of the payoffs multiplied by the probabilities of the payoffs. So in the case of the second option above, the expected value is a million dollars multiplied by 90 percent plus nothing multiplied by ten percent — 0.9($1000,000) + 0.1($0), or $900,000.

That's $50,000 more than $850,000. So by all rational means, you should choose to take the second option. After all, odds of 9 to 1 are very good, and you're almost certain to win the million dollars.

On the other hand, if you take the second option, there's always that small chance that you could end up winning nothing, which means that, not only did you not win anything, you also passed up the opportunity to get $850,000 certain.

As a consequence, virtually all people opt to take the $850,000 and forgo the opportunity to win a million dollars. The possibility that, if you choose the second option, you could end up with nothing is a large loss to which you're averse, and you opt to play it safe by taking the $850,000 certain, even though the second option has an expected value of $900,000. Your aversion to the possible large loss determines your choice.

The fundamental characteristic of this class of loss aversion is that you have a choice between the certainty of a very large benefit and the chance to realize an even larger benefit at the, admittedly small, risk of ending up with nothing. In this case, your aversion to the possible large loss leads you to choose $850,000 certain over the chance of gaining an even greater amount, no matter how good the chances are. (K 280,285)

Now, let's turn the situation around. You can choose between losing $850,000 for certain or taking a gamble where there's a 90 percent chance of losing a million dollars and a ten percent chance of not losing anything.

Here the expected value of the uncertain option is still a million dollars multiplied by 90 percent plus nothing multiplied by ten percent — 0.9($1000,000) + 0.1($0), or $900,000. That's $50,000 more than the certain loss of $850,000. So by all rational means, you should choose the first option.

But the idea of losing $850,000 is so unbearable that most people opt to take a chance on being able to avoid any loss, even though the odds are 9 to 1 that they're going to lose, not $850,000, but a million dollars.

The classic example of this kind of loss aversion is the poker hand where you start out with a reasonably good set of cards, but as the hand progresses, another player improves his cards to the point where it's evident that the cards that you're holding are a sure loser. However, you've already put so much money into the pot that you're reluctant to fold and take the loss.

So instead, you stay in the hand and continue to put money in the pot on the slim chance that you may improve your cards to the point where you can win the pot. This behavior makes no sense.

Money put in the pot is a sunk cost and shouldn't be taken into consideration when making subsequent decisions. But the money already in the pot is hard to forget, and throwing good money after bad is common.

Another example of this kind of situation is when a residential real estate bubble bursts. The price that a homeowner's house would have brought at the top of the market is a reference point, and accepting anything less looks like a loss. So the homeowner holds out for a better price than the market offers and finds that he can't sell his house at all. A person who won't accept loss takes actions that worsen his position. (Po 101,133)

A third example is the nation that continues a war long past the point where defeat is almost certain, because it's too difficult to accept defeat (K 319). For example, any time after Antietam, when it became apparent that the South wasn't going to win the war, it could have thrown in the towel and curtailed the drain on its resources. But that was too big a loss to be considered, so it fought on until it was devastated.

The fundamental characteristic of this class of loss aversion is that you have a choice between a certain, large loss and a remote possibility of avoiding the loss, even though pursuing the remote possibility will almost inevitably lead to an even larger loss. In this case, your loss aversion leads you to choose the remote possibility of avoiding a large loss at the expense of a course of action that will, almost inevitably, lead to an even larger loss. (K 280,285)

A third type of loss aversion is exemplified by residential house insurance. If you own the house in which you live, the chances are that it represents a good part, if not the bulk, of your assets.

Under such conditions, if your house were destroyed, the loss would be devastating, a loss that you wouldn't want to experience. As a consequence, each year, you pay an insurance company a premium so that, if your house is destroyed, the insurance company will reimburse you for the value of your loss.

But the chance that your house will be destroyed is extremely low. If you multiply your house's value by this low probability, you'll arrive at an amount that's less than the sum of the present value of the premiums that you're going to pay the insurance company over the course of your life in the probable case where nothing bad happens to your house.

The difference is what gives the insurance company its profit. Your aversion to the possibility of the destruction of your house leads you to insure against this possibility, despite the fact that, from a purely financial point of view, it's a poor choice.

The fundamental characteristic of this class of loss aversion is that you have a choice between the remote possibility of experiencing a devastating loss and the certainty of avoiding the loss by assuming a cost that's more than the expected value of the loss but much less than the loss itself. In this case, your loss aversion leads you to choose the certainty of avoiding a large loss at the expense of paying more than the expected value of the loss in exchange for the certainty.

Aversion to a loss is an impediment to conflict resolution. If you conceive of your concessions as losses, whenever you make a concession, you're going to consider yourself as getting the worse of the deal. And your opponent is going to reach the same conclusion with respect to himself. The result is that both sides are reluctant to make concessions, the opposite of compromise. (H 75)

The Present versus The Future

We favor the present over the future, as indicated by the adage that a bird in hand is worth two in the bush, even if the future has more value than the present. There's a sociobiological reason for this phenomenon. When you're a hunter-gatherer, what you can get now is worth more than almost anything that you could gain in the future.

In the present, we know what we're dealing with, but the future is iffy and may not be favorable. So, in general, choosing the present over the future is a good idea, but it can result in choosing short-term gains at the price of forfeiting large benefits in the future.

The predilection to favor current gains over future ones seems to explain why people charge more on their credit cards than they're able to pay off at the end of the month. Being able to take advantage of that bargain, even if it's for something that you don't really need, is more compelling than the future requirement to pay interest that's going to eat up any gains that you might have made by taking advantage of the sale.

Favoring present pleasure over future pain might also have been involved in the creation of the subprime mortgage. Hey, why worry about ballooning interest payments in the future? I can move into a house RIGHT NOW.

The development of the prefrontal cortex, where rational thought takes place, occurs rather late in life. It's doesn't reach full maturity until the early 20s.

This creates a problem when it comes to dealing with teenagers. Their emotions are at full throttle while their rationality is still stunted.

For example, how do you get high school students to apply themselves to their studies? Emphasizing the importance of getting a high school diploma doesn't cut much ice. Graduation date is a long way away but getting together with your buddies is something that you can do right now.

Some states, such as West Virginia, have approached this problem by revoking the driver's license of students who aren't performing academically. Not getting a diploma is far in the future, but not having wheels is happening right now. (L 114)

When rewards are immediate and costs long-term or when costs are immediate and rewards long-term, temptation comes into play. In the case of 401(k)s, both factors are in operation. Not signing up involves no reduction in take-home pay, and a financially cramped retirement is a long way away. Signing up involves an immediate decrease in take-home pay, while a comfortable retirement is a long way away.

Temptation operates in other critical areas. Eating all of that yummy food is immediately rewarding. Getting fat, with all of its attendant medical problems, is longer term.

Exercise is costly. It requires a current expenditure in time and effort. The benefits of a longer, healthier life are longer term. (T 73)

Framing

A decision can be based on the way in which the situation, to which the decision relates, is presented, or framed.

For example, given the choice of buying something that comes in three prices, people tend to buy the version with the middle price. Wine stores take advantage of this tendency by arranging their wines by price.

For example, you'll find the chardonnays lined up from lowest to highest price. The wine store does this because it knows that most people aren't going to buy the highest priced wine but also don't want to appear cheap, so they go for the middle, where the biggest markup is. (A 4) The way in which the situation is framed influences the decision.

Here's another example of how framing influences buying habits. A restaurant can improve its profit by adding a high priced item to its menu.

Few people will order the highest price meal on the menu. But they do tend to order the second highest priced item, the price of which can be manipulated so that it has the highest profit margin. (A 4)

Also, Coach offers a $7000 alligator handbag. Each Coach flagship store carries one or two such bags.

Coach doesn't expect to sell these bags. But their prominent display in the store makes its $2000 ostrich handbag seem to be more reasonable priced. (Po 158)

Try this exercise. You paid $10 for a ticket to a show. When you get to the theater, you discover that you've lost the ticket. Would you buy another ticket?

Now try this one. You go to a theater to see a play for which the ticket price is $10. When you step up to the ticket booth, you discover that you've lost a $10 bill. Would you still buy a ticket?

More people say that they'd buy a ticket at the ticket booth in the second situation than they would in the first. The explanation again is framing.

People keep mental accounts. In the first case, the initial ticket purchase price of $10 was entered into the "ticket purchase" account. When it came time to replace the lost ticket, a second $10 purchase would have to be entered into the "ticket purchase" account, which would bring the cost of the show up to $20 for a $10 ticket, something many people choose not to do. In the second case, the lost $10 would be debited to the general cash account and buying the ticket would still cost only $10.

All obfuscation, because the two situations are identical. In both cases, you've lost $10 and the only pertinent question is whether you want to spend $10 to see the show.

Framing can be used for the benefit of both society and the people involved. For example, if when you're hired, you're enrolled in the company's 401(k) plan unless you opt out, more people will participate than will if, when you're hired, you won't participate in the 401(k) plan unless you opt in. (T 8,83)

Organ donation happens more often if, when you sign up for a driver's license, you're automatically enrolled in the organ donation program unless you opt out than if, when you get your license, you're not enrolled unless you opt in. In Austria, when the default case is participation, almost everyone is part of the program. In Germany, where the opposite is the case, participation is 12 percent. In Sweden, where you're in unless you opt out, participation is 86 percent. In Denmark, where you have to opt in, it's four percent. Similar cultural backgrounds, but participation is a function of the way in which the choice is framed. (K 373)

Words and other stimuli prime mental processes that influence subsequent thoughts or actions. (Po 94) For example, people who are asked if they're going to vote (that's it — no pressure, no exhortation, nothing but a question) are more inclined to vote, by about 25 percent, than those who aren't asked. (T 69,70)

When numerical values are involved, priming is known as anchoring. Here's an example.

Suppose that you have to guess the population of Milwaukee. If you're from Chicago, with a population of three million, you say, "Well, Milwaukee is a city, but it's smaller than Chicago. Maybe its population is a million."

However, if you're from Green Bay, with a population of about 100 thousand, you say, "Well, Milwaukee is larger than Green Bay. Maybe its population is 300 thousand."

Actually, Milwaukee's population is about 600 thousand. (T 23) The population of where you're from serves as a reference point, and from this reference point, you adjust to arrive at a number that sounds reasonable to you.

Suppose that you're on the verge of buying a $25 pen when someone tells you that, if you walk 15 minutes down the street, you can get the pen for $18. Most people will take the time to buy the lower priced pen.

Now suppose that you're on the verge of buying a $255 suit when someone tells you that, by walking down the street for 15 minutes, you can get the same suit for $248. Most people won't bother.

These people are using the price of the purchase as a reference point and are comparing the value of the savings to this anchor, which is irrelevant but frames the decision situation. The relevant question is: Is walking down the street for 15 minutes worth $7 to you? (A 19,20)

True, the percentage savings on the pen is $7 divided by $25, or 28 percent, while the percentage savings on the suit is $7 divided by $255, or just 2.7 percent. But concentrating on the percentage savings is a delusion. In both cases, what you save is $7.

Markdowns are an example of how marketers can take advantage of framing to encourage people to buy. For example, suppose that a price tag reads "Regular Price $48, On Sale for $40".

This is a price reduction come-on encouraging people to buy. But many customers have no idea of what the regular price should be, and the advertised "regular price" may, in fact, be a markup. (Po 191) However, it serves as a reference point when deciding whether to buy.

If the plaintiff in a liability lawsuit prevails, he's compensated for the expenses that he has incurred as a result of his mistreatment by the defendant plus an additional award to compensate him for his pain and suffering. It's up to the jury to decide what the appropriate compensatory award should be.

Theoretically, the amount of the award should vary with the extent of the pain and suffering. But there's no objective way to scale a monetary award to an intensity of suffering.

As a result, the amount that a jury decides to award is typically determined by the amount for which the plaintiff asks. So the recommended approach is to ask for a lot.

The jury won't give the plaintiff everything they ask for, but if they ask for a lot, they'll get more than they would if they had asked for less. The amount asked for is a reference point from which the jury adjusts. The more you ask for, the more you get.

The rule applies in any bargaining situation. And it pays to get your bid in first. The person who names the first number establishes the stronger reference point. (Po 1,17,18,19,110,204,211)

Confirmation Bias

We give weight to information that supports our opinions and downplay data contrary to our opinions. This is the confirmation bias. It causes us to overlook significant information.

Here's an example of how confirmation bias works. You're told that you'll be given a string of three numbers that follows a rule and that your job is to determine what the rule is.

You're to conduct your investigation into the nature of the rule by proposing other three-number strings, and for each proposed string, you'll be told whether or not the string conforms to the rule. You can continue this investigation for as long as you want, but when you become convinced that you've determined the rule, you can state the rule. You'll then be told whether or not you have correctly identified the rule, and if you're incorrect, you'll be told what the rule really is.

Here's the string of numbers that you're given.

2 4 6

Try it. What string of numbers would you propose to test the rule that you think that the given string follows?

If you're like most people, the rule that most readily pops into your head is that the string is a series of even numbers increasing by two. To confirm this hypothesis, you might propose a string such as:

8 10 12

In response, you're told that the proposed string does, indeed, conform to the rule. You're encouraged. So, you might propose something really wild, like:

116 118 120

Again, you'd be told that your proposed string conforms. If you suspect that things might not be quite what they seem, you might decide to try out the idea that maybe the rule is just that the numbers have to increase by two and can be even or odd. So you might propose:

1 3 5

Again, confirmation. By now your confidence is overwhelming. So you state your rule: Numbers increasing by two.

But it turns out that you're wrong. The rule is: Any string of increasing numbers. So 1 2 3 follows the rule, as does 16 128 405. −6 -4 -2 even follows the rule.

All of the way through this exercise, you mostly sought evidence that would confirm the hypothesis that you had in mind. What you need to do, to progress in determining the nature of the rule, is to seek out evidence that would disprove your hypothesis.

You took a first step in this direction when you proposed odd numbers rather than even ones. That disproved the hypothesis that the rule involved only even numbers.

But you didn't follow through. You then should have tried a string such as 1 2 3. Confirmation of this proposed string would disprove the idea that the numbers have to be separated by two. If you had then tried -6 -4 -2, confirmation would have disproved the idea that the numbers have to be positive.

But it wouldn't be until you proposed something like 3 2 1 and received the information that this string *doesn't* conform to the rule, that you'd have started to get a fix on what the rule might be. It's the negation of hypotheses that leads to the development of better hypotheses.

The way to buttress a proposition isn't to seek out confirming information. Instead, you should look for evidence that throws doubt on the proposition. It's from the continuing failure of such a search to turn up any such evidence that support for the proposition grows. (To 139)

Here's another example. You have a deck of cards. Each card has a letter on one side and a number on the other. The hypothesis is that, if a card has a vowel on one side, then it has an odd number on the other side.

You're given four cards: B, E, 4 and 7. The question is: Which cards do you have to turn over to see if you can disprove the hypothesis?

The B card is pretty easy. There's no point in turning it over, since whatever's on the other side, it's irrelevant as far as the hypothesis is concerned.

But you want to turn over the E card, because if it has an even number on the other side, the hypothesis is disproved. Most people get this.

They then want to turn over the 7 card, to see if it has a vowel on the other side. I was one of them.

But turning over the 7 card proves nothing. The hypothesis is that, if a card has a vowel on one side, then it has an odd number on the other. It's not that, if a card has an odd number, then it has a vowel on the other. It could have a consonant and not disprove the hypothesis.

The other card that you have to turn over is the 4 card, because if it has a vowel on the other side, then the hypothesis is disproved.

Availability

Here's an example of availability. The question is: Which is greater: The number of words having "n" as their next to last letter or the number of words ending in "ing"?

Most people go for the "ing". That's because of availability.

We can easily conceive of a lot of words ending in "ing". It's harder to think of words with an "n" in the next to last letter.

However, here our instinct has, once more, led us astray. All of the words ending in "ing" have an "n" in their next to last letter and the probability is high that there's at least one word not ending in "ing" that, nevertheless, has an "n" as its next to last letter. So the better bet is that there are more words with "n" in the next to last letter. (Ml 28)

The Halo Effect

If a person knows a lot about one subject, there's a tendency to believe that he knows a lot about everything. (S 275)

Remembering Pleasant and Painful Experiences

You'll remember any given experience as either pleasant or painful on the basis of the combination of the high point and final point of the experience. Duration of the experience isn't a factor. (K 380,383)

For example, if you take a two-week vacation, you have a particularly pleasant experience during the vacation, and the vacation ends on a high note, you'll remember the overall vacation as a pleasant one, even though, during the bulk of the vacation, nothing notable happened. Similarly, if you had a really bad experience during the vacation and it ended on a sour note, you'll remember it as an unpleasant vacation, even though, during the bulk of the vacation, things went well enough.

Daniel Kahneman, winner of the Nobel Prize in economics for his work with Amos Tversky on how people aren't always rational when it comes to making economic decisions, and his colleagues demonstrated this fact with a telling experiment. Participants went through two trials during which they immersed a hand, up to the wrist, in water that was cold enough to cause moderate but tolerable pain. (K 382)

During the first trial, the water was kept at a temperature of 14 degrees Celsius and the participants held their hand in the water for 60 seconds. During the second trial, the participants held their hand in the water for 90 seconds. During the first 60 seconds, the water was kept at 14 degrees Celsius. At that point, the person conducting the experiment surreptitiously opened a valve that allowed the water to warm up by one degree. (K 382)

Before beginning the experiment, the participants were told that the experiment would consist of three trials. At the end of the second trial, the participants were given a choice for the third trial. They could repeat the first trial or they could repeat the second one.

Eighty percent of the participants chose to repeat the second trial. They thus chose to experience 30 seconds of needless pain simply because, in the second trial, the ending experience was less painful than the ending experience of the first trial. (The third trial was never conducted.) (K 382,383,408)

Our inclination is to favor a short period of intense joy over a long period of moderate happiness and to be inclined to give up the opportunity for a long happy period if it's anticipated that it will end badly (K 409). Not a good way to conduct your life (K 385).

Planning

When planning a project, the tendency is to look at the particular project and figure out what's going to happen and how long it will take. A better approach would be to look at similar projects that have been undertaken in the past and see what happened to them and how long it took for them to be completed.

The second approach would provide a baseline for your planning, which can then be modified to take into consideration the particulars of your project. Concentration solely on the particular project tends to result in confining consideration to the best-case scenario, which means that the contingencies that characterize projects are given short shrift. (K 247,248,251,252)

Confining planning to the best-case scenario generally results in unjustified optimism (K 253). No one getting married believes that they're going to get divorced. Yet the sad, hard fact is that half of marriages end in divorce. (T 32)

Undue optimism may also explain why nations go to war and why people litigate and start small businesses (K 253). The chances that a small business in the US will survive for five years are about 35 percent (K 256). Sixty percent of restaurants go out of business within three years. In general, people make more money selling their skills to employers than they do by going into business for themselves. (K 257).

Small Samples

We tend to over rely on small samples.

A study of the incidence of kidney cancer in the 3141 counties of the US revealed that the incidence of kidney cancer is lowest in rural counties. It easy to see why. The low incidence was undoubtedly the result of clean rural living — no air or water pollution and access to fresh food with no additives.

But the study also showed that the incidence of kidney cancer is highest in rural counties. Once more, the result can be easily explained. The high incidence must be the result of the poverty of the rural life style — no access to good medical care, high fat diet, and too much alcohol and tobacco.

In fact, the key factor here is that rural counties have small populations. With small populations, the rural counties have a better statistical chance of exhibiting extreme outcomes, chances that are reduced when sample size is increased. (K 109,110,111)

The fact that two completely contradictory facts can each be so easily rationalized serves as an admonition to not jump to conclusions. Going off halfcocked can lead to pernicious consequences, as the following case demonstrates.

In a survey of 1662 schools in Pennsylvania it was found that six of the top 50 schools were small, an overrepresentation by a factor of four. As a result, the Gates Foundation made an investment of $1.7 billion in the creation of small schools, sometimes by splitting large schools into smaller units.

The Foundation was joined in this effort by a dozen other prominent institutions, such as the Annenberg Foundation and the Pew Charitable Trust. Also participating was the US Department of Education's Smaller Learning Communities Program. (K 117)

A deeper investigation would have revealed that, not only do the best schools tend to be small, so do the bad schools. Small schools aren't better or poorer on average, they're just more variable. (K 118)

The moral of the story is straightforward – don't trust small samples. They can lead you astray.

Randomness plays a role in determining how big a sample you need to make an informed decision. The more the randomness, the bigger the sample that you need.

For example, if you're wondering about sprinter ranking, you have to observe only a few trials to determine who the fastest sprinters are, because they beat the slower ones every time. Randomness (or luck or chance, as randomness is generally referred to when speaking of sports) plays little part in a sprint.

But in a sport where luck plays a bigger part, you need a larger number of trials to determine which individual or team is the best. (Ma 26). For example, the World Series is a farce. The teams that make it to the World Series tend to be more or less equal. Even if one team has an unusually large 55-45 advantage, assuming that luck is normally distributed (which seems to be reasonable), it would take 269 games to determine the better team with a five percent level of confidence. (M)

Too small a sample can lead to what's known as premature closure. After looking at a few cases, a conclusion is reached and further investigation is suspended, even though looking at more cases would have revealed that the conclusion is invalid. (G 185).

Statistics

Statistics is a relatively new area of study and, while understood intellectually, isn't built into our psyche. At an instinctual level, we have trouble dealing with statistics. We're more inclined to be influenced by outstanding examples, no matter how exceptional.

Again, this can lead to error. For example, because we read about female celebrities who have children when they're in their 40s, we believe that it's not unusual for a woman to have a baby when she's in her 40s, despite the fact that, in general, women in their 40s have difficulty having children and, most commonly, fail to do so.

Ellen Peters, a psychologist at Ohio State, gave research volunteers a chance to win money by randomly selecting a jellybean from one of two jars. When volunteers selected a red jellybean, they won.

One jar contained 100 jellybeans, nine of which were red. The jar was labeled "nine percent red beans". The other jar contained ten jellybeans, one of which was red. It was labeled "ten percent red beans".

Even though, clearly, a ten percent chance is better than a nine percent one, many of the volunteers were conflicted, because one bottle had nine red beans in it while the other had only one. (U 140,141)

Regression to the Mean

One of the things that Kahneman did in his career was to teach flight instructors in the Israeli Air Force about the psychology of effective training, during which he told them about the training principle that rewards for improved performance work better than punishments for mistakes.

The instructors disagreed. They pointed out that, when they praised a cadet for an exceptional performance, they generally found that, the next time, the cadet didn't perform as well, while when they castigated a cadet for poor execution, the next time, the cadet typically improved. (K 175)

As Kahneman pointed out in his book, *Thinking, Fast and Slow*, the instructors were both right and wrong. They were right about the cadets' performance, but they were wrong about the reason for it.

After an exceptionally good performance, regardless of whether or not the cadet was praised, on his next venture, he typically returned to a more average level of performance. The same was true for the cadet with the poor performance. He had a bad day, and whether or not he was chewed out, his subsequence performance was usually more average. (K 175,176)

This is an example of regression to the mean, which means that behavior tends to fluctuate but averages out to a mean. It's a statistical fact with which we have trouble dealing. Our inclination is to look for causes to explain behavior. Regression to the mean has an explanation but doesn't have a cause. (K 182)

Once more, the combination of skill and luck involved in the activity being performed is a determining factor in the regression to the mean. If performance is overwhelmingly the result of skill, then the skillful participant will be able to consistently keep his performance well above the mean. In this case, you can predict the participant's future behavior on the basis of his past performance.

But if luck is the dominant factor, then any deviation from the mean is, almost invariably, the result of a lucky, or unlucky, fluke, and it's unlikely to continue. Here your better predictor of future performance is average performance. (Ma 28,206,207)

The Bystander Effect

The more the number of people who witness an emergency, the less likely it is that anyone will intervene to help. The explanation seems to be that, the larger the number of witnesses, the more each witness excuses himself from doing anything because he thinks that someone else will step in. (Z 315)

Fair or Selfish

To determine whether we have an innate sense of fairness or are fundamentally selfish, psychologists have developed some games.

One of these games is the ultimatum game, which goes like this. A "proposer" is given an amount of money, typically, $10. He has to split this money with a "responder".

The character of the split is up to the proposer. He can split the money 50-50, 60-40, whatever he wants, ranging from giving it all away to keeping it all for himself.

The kicker is that the responder gets to decide whether to accept the proposer's offer. If he does, then both keep whatever the proposer's split provides for. However, if he rejects the proposal, then neither gets anything. (Po 110,111)

When the game is played, the most common proposal is 50-50. But rationally, even a 90-10 split should be acceptable to the responder. After all, $1 is better than nothing.

But in fact, that isn't the way responders react. They tend to accept as little as $3, but a $2 offer is just too little. They'd rather not get anything than let the proposer get away with such an unfair deal.

The next question is: Do proposers who make acceptable offers do so because they're responding to a sense of fairness, or are they just trying to frame the game so that they assure that responders don't turn down their proposals? The dictator game provides answers (more than one) to this question.

In the original dictator game, the proposer proposed the split and the responder took whatever split the proposer proposed. The responder couldn't reject the proposal.

Under these conditions, proposers continued to make acceptable offers. Chalk up one for a sense of fairness.

But wait. A refinement was then introduced.

Each proposer received an envelope that generally held ten singles and ten bill sized sheets of blank paper. In privacy, he then removed ten slips from the envelope. He could remove all ten of the singles, all ten of the blank sheets, or some combination of singles and blanks. The envelope was then returned to an attendant, who delivered it to a responder.

Some of the original envelopes contained just 20 blanks, in which case, the proposer's only course of action was to remove ten of the blanks. So a responder never knew which proposer prepared the envelope that the responder received, and if the envelope contained ten blanks, the responder didn't know whether this was a choice of the proposer or if the proposer simply had no choice.

Under these new circumstances, 60 percent of the proposers kept all ten of the singles. So the proposers in the original game weren't responding to a sense of fairness. Instead, they were trying to avoid being identified as greedy. (Po 117,118,119)

Indications are that we're better off maintaining positive peer pressure and an effective police force than we'd be if we depended on people's good will. In the meantime, we should continue to, in every way possible, encourage people to do the right thing.

Tribalism

We're tribal. We herd. And with good reason. Getting together with other people increases the probability of both surviving and surviving comfortably. This tendency leads to a constellation of behaviors related to decision making: conventional wisdom, peer pressure, obedience to authority, and xenophobia.

Conventional Wisdom

We tend to go along with the crowd. And we do so for sound sociobiological reasons. When belonging to a group is essential to survival, it doesn't pay to be disagreeable.

However, this inclination can get us into trouble. Here's an example of conventional wisdom: It's believed that bottled water is superior to tap water, although tap water is perfectly safe. In fact, federal standards for tap water are more stringent and more strictly enforced than they are for bottled water. Nevertheless, people continue to buy bottled water, because conventional wisdom says that its safer.

Another example of conventional wisdom is: If something costs more, it's better.

Yet one blind taste test concluded that Smirnoff, a relatively cheap vodka, was the best tasting, favored over, among other vodkas, Gray Goose and Ketel One. (Ml 214,215). People taking a blind taste test run by *The Wall Street Journal* concluded that, among five wines, the best tasting was a Gallo product, by far the lowest priced wine in the test. Conversely, when novice wine drinkers sampled five wines priced from $5 to $90 a bottle, they expressed a preference for the more expensive ones, even though the wine in the five bottles was all the same (I 152).

The Lancome and Maybelline brands of cosmetics both belong to L'Oreal. Their matte foundations are made in the same factories and are nearly identical in composition. Yet even though L'Oreal sells Maybelline New York's Dream Matte Mousse Foundation for $8.99, it still has no trouble getting rid of Lancome Magique Matte Soft-Matte Perfecting Mousse Makeup at $37. (I 156)

Peer Pressure

In addition to wanting to get along with the tribe, another force working for conformity is peer pressure. Perhaps the most impressive demonstration of peer pressure is the following experiment.

A group of people are repeatedly shown two lines, one of which is longer than the other and are asked which is longer. Actually, only one member of the group is the subject of the study. All of the other members are confederates of the investigator, and sometimes, they identify the shorter line as the longer one.

Ultimately, most subjects go along with the group decision. One of these studies determined that, if the subject had just one other person who agreed with him, the extent to which he went along with the group decreased to one fourth. (Z 264)

Peer pressure can be a good thing. It inclines people toward behaving in the way that society thinks that they should. But as the above experiment indicates, it can be used for nefarious purposes, such as encouraging drug use.

Obedience to Authority

We obey authority. We come by this tendency naturally. When belonging to a group is essential, it doesn't pay to mess with the alpha dog.

Again, this inclination is positive in that it contributes to group cohesiveness. But this inclination also gives authoritarians the latitude that they need to undermine the principles that experience has indicated are essential for beneficial government.

The most explicit demonstration of the extent to which obedience to authority can be pernicious is an experiment carried out by Stanley Milgram. In 1961, he posted newspaper advertisements in New Haven and Bridgeport for male volunteers to participate in an experiment to study the effects of punishment on learning. (M 26) Pay was $4.50 (M 28).

When a volunteer reached Milgram's Yale laboratory, he was met by a stern-looking experimenter in lab coat, who led the volunteer into a testing room. There the volunteer was introduced to Mr. Wallace, who, the experimenter explained, was another volunteer who had been randomly chosen to be the "learner" in the experiment. The volunteer was going to be the "teacher". (M 26) Unknown to the volunteer, Wallace was actually a participant in the experiment.

While the volunteer watched, Wallace was strapped into a chair to "reduce movement" and an electrode was attached to his arm. The volunteer and the experimenter then went into another room, where the volunteer could communicate with Wallace through an intercom. The volunteer sat in front of a switchboard with a long row of switcches labeled with increasing amounts of voltage, beginning on the left at 15 volts and ending on the right at 450 volts. (M 26,27)

The volunteer was to read Wallace a long list of word pairs, such as "dance" and "boy". When he was finished, he was then to randomly pick one of the words in one of the word pairs, say the word to Wallace, and Wallace was expected to reply with the matching word of the pair. (M 26,27)

If Wallace came up with the right word, the volunteer selected another word, and the process continued. If Wallace came up with the wrong word or if, after a specified time limit, there was no answer, the volunteer was instructed to throw a switch on the switchboard, starting with the switch on the left. (M 27)

Throwing a switch was supposed to, through the electrode on Wallace's arm, administer an electric shock to Wallace of the strength indicated on the switch label. Actually, the whole thing was a sham. Wallace received no shock, but he did know when a switch was thrown and which switch it was. The volunteer, of course, knew nothing of the artifice. He was told by the experimenter that the shocks were "painful, but not harmful." (M 27)

Each time Wallace delivered a wrong answer, the volunteer was to throw another switch, progressing though the voltage levels from left to right. After the first few shocks, Wallace could be heard to grunt when the next shock was delivered. A few more shocks, and he began crying out in pain. He started to complain that his heart was bothering him. (M 27)

As the process continued, each successive shock was met by long, ragged screams. Finally, Wallace shouted out, "Let me out of here! *Let me out*! LET ME OUT!" After that, he fell silent. (M 27)

At some point, the volunteer would ask the experimenter if they shouldn't stop. The experimenter explained that the volunteer could stop at any time, and he'd receive his $4.50. But, the experimenter went on to explain, "The experiment requires that you continue." (M 28) He assured the volunteer that, if anything went wrong, he'd take full responsibility (M 32).

Half of the volunteers carried on the experiment right to the end, administering progressively greater shocks to an unresponsive Wallace until a top level of 450 volts was reached (M 28).

We must resist the tendency to defer to authority whenever authority asks us to do something that violates our conscience.

Xenophobia

The most deleterious result of tribalism is that it engenders the attitude that it's us against them. They're not our kind. They're inferior, degenerate, and not worthy of our respect. We discriminate against them. We put them down and raise barriers to keep them away from us. We enjoy subjecting them to indignities and injury. The more we dominate others, the more we misuse them.

The clearest demonstration that misusing people over whom we have dominance is a normal human behavior is an experiment carried out by Philip Zimbardo, a professor at Stamford, in 1971, an experiment known as the Stamford Prison Experiment. Zimbardo outfitted the basement of the Stamford psychological department as a prison.

Both the guards and the prisoners at Zimbardo's "prison" were college students who had volunteered to participate in the experiment, for which they'd be paid $15 a day (P 14), and they were screened in advance for "normalcy" (no criminal record, no emotional or physical disability, no intellectual or social disadvantage or advantage, passage of various personality tests), and they were randomly assigned to their roles by flipping a coin (P 4).

Zimbardo's briefing of his guards was as follows. There couldn't be any physical abuse. But the prisoners were to have no privacy, there would be constant surveillance, the prisoners would be permitted to do only what the guards told them, they would wear uniforms with numbers on them, and they would be addressed by number only, no names.

The idea was to create a feeling of powerlessness in the prisoners. Zimbardo wanted to see what they'd do under such circumstances. However, it was the behavior of the guards that surprised him. (Z 20,55,196)

Almost immediately, the guards began harassing the prisoners, requiring them to engage in all kinds of pointless drills, berating them for purported failure to perform, punishing them by taking away their blankets, pillows, and cots, and forcing them to engage in demeaning activity such as cleaning the toilet bowls with their bare hands and having them simulate sodomy. By the second day, a prisoner had to be released because he was in emotional disarray.

By the fourth day, another prisoner had broken down and had to be released. On the fifth day, two more prisoners had to be excused. Although the experiment had originally been scheduled to run for two weeks, by the sixth day it was spiraling out of control and was shut down (Z 78,107,159,160,178).

Zimbardo also served as an expert witness for Staff Sergeant Ivan Frederick II, the MP who was in charge of the night shift on Tiers 1A and 1B at Abu Ghraib. The prisoner interrogation room at Abu Ghraib was in Tier 1A. The interrogators explicitly asked the MPs to soften up the prisoners to assist the interrogators in doing their job. The MPs received no supervision. The only direction that they got from their higher ups was that they wanted the prisoners to be broken so that interrogation would be more successful (Z 331,349,352,358,383).

Even though it was against policy, the interrogators allowed the MPs to observe interrogations. After seeing what took place during interrogations, what the MPs did on the prison floor seemed like child's play.

In his book, *The Lucifer Effect*, Zimbardo says that how the MPs treated the prisoners at Abu Ghraib is banal. Given a situation in which misuse can be practiced with impunity, it will. This was most tragically demonstrated in the Holocaust.

If we want to avoid these horrendous situations, whenever one group is in a position of domination over others, such as in prisons, there have to be structural safeguards in place to prevent the development of misuse (Z x,xi,9,10,211,226,445,446).

The Rational Mind

For millennia, our instincts have contributed to our survival, even if, on occasion, they lead us astray. Trusting your gut is a time-tested fallback position. But we now have a rational mind that can help us recognize these biases and consciously avoid the pitfalls that they can open up for us.

However, we shouldn't be overly proud of or confident in the ability of our rational mind to unerringly guide us in reliable ways. Our rational mind can get us into just as much trouble as our instincts.

For example, suppose that you have a blinking light. Sometimes it blinks red, sometimes green.

Suppose further that there are two buttons, one red, the other green. If you press the red button and, the next time the light blinks, it blinks red, you get rewarded. If it blinks green, there's no reward.

Similarly with the green button. If you press it and the light blinks green, you get a reward. If it blinks red, no reward.

Finally, suppose that, 60 percent of the time, the light blinks red.

A white rat will soon figure out that the light blinks red more often than it blinks green, and from that point on, it will just sit on the red button and settle for a return 60 percent of the time.

In contrast, when we look at the light, we think, "I don't have to settle for 60 percent. If I can figure out the pattern that the light is following, I can get 100 percent."

This is our rational mind talking. The rational mind is a pattern seeker.

Fortunately, a lot of the world follows a pattern, so our search for patterns has allowed us to gain considerable control over our world. And if the light in our experiment is following a pattern and we can figure it out, we can, indeed, win all of the time.

However, if the blinking of the light is random, and some significant things in this world do occur randomly, we aren't going to be able to realize a 100 percent return, and there's a distinct possibility that we may not do as well as the white rat, which is something that you might keep in mind the next time that you're considering investing in the stock market.

Sources

(A) Ariely, Dan, *Predictably Irrational* (HarperCollins 2008)

(G) Groopman, Jerome, *How Doctors Think* (Houghton Mifflin 2007)

(H) Harris, Sam, *The Moral Landscape* (Simon & Schuster 2010)

(I) Iyengar, Sheena, *The Art of Choosing* (Hachette 2010)

(J) Jay, Meg, *The Defining Decade* (Hachette 2012)

(K) Kahneman, Daniel, *Thinking, Fast and Slow* (Farrar, Straus and Giroux 2011)

(Ka) Kaplan, Michael and Ellen, *Bozo Sapiens* (Bloomsbury 2009)

(L) Lehrer, Jonah, *How We Decide* (Houghton Mifflin 2009)

(M) Marsh, Abigail *The Fear Factor* (Hachette 2017)

(Ma) Mauboussin, Michael J., *The Success Equation* (Harvard Business School Publishing (2012)

(Ml) Mlodinow, Leonard, *The Drunkard's Walk* (Random House 2008)

(P) Pearl, Robert *Mistreated* (Hatchette 2017)

(Po) Poundstone, William, *Priceless* (Farrar, Straus and Giroux 2010)

(S) Shermer, Michael, *The Believing Brain* (Henry Holt 2011)

(Sh) Sherwood, Ben, *The Survivors Club* (Hachette 2009)

(T) Thaler, Richard H. and Sunstein, Cass R., *Nudge* (Yale U 2008)

(Th) Thaler, Richard H. *Misbehaving* (W. W. Norton 2015).

(To) Tough, Paul, *How Children Succeed* (Houghton Mifflin Harcourt 2012)

(U) Ubel, Peter A., *Critical Decisions* (HarperCollins 2012)

(Z) Zimbardo, Philip, *The Lucifer Effect* (Random House 2007)

CHAPTER SIX

Love

We become attached to other people.

There's mother love. Instinctively, a mother is drawn to and wants to fondle, nurture and protect her newborn child. She comes by this instinct for good evolutionary reasons. If Mom didn't look after her cubs, we wouldn't be here.

There's an instinctive desire to view our relatives with favor and to be interested in their well-being. As my father used to say, blood is thicker than water.

We have an inclination to enter into relationships with people whom we've decided are special. "Every so often, someone comes along and touches your life in a special way." In these relationships, we want to help our partners when they're in need, console them when they're distressed, share their joy, sympathize with them when they're sad, encourage and support them in their endeavors, and in general, just be there. These relationships last when there's reciprocity and the partners accept each other as they are. "I like you just the way you are." Neither partner wants to change the other, and they don't subject each other to ridicule, scorn or disrespect.

If such a relationship doesn't involve sex, it's friendship, which is rare, but happens.

If the relationship involves sex, it's romantic love. And that's as common as the grass.

No one is perfect. We all make mistakes. When you inadvertently hurt your partner, the appropriate thing to do is to offer a genuine apology for the transgression. And the appropriate response to an apology is to forgive and forget.

However, one can't fall into the habit of thinking that transgressions are no big deal, because all that you have to do is apologize and you'll be forgiven. There's a limit to the degree to which transgressions can be tolerated. After being forgiven, you should undertake, with renewed determination, to see that the transgression doesn't happen again.

CHAPTER SEVEN
Money

Consider two people. Suppose that they both want both venison and corn.

Each can spend part of their time hunting deer and the rest of their time raising corn. Each consumes the fruits of their hunting and farming. These people live in a *subsistence economy.*

As an alternative to a subsistence economy, one person can devote himself to hunting and the other to farming. The hunter can exchange venison for corn with the farmer. The hunter and farmer then make up an *exchange economy*, an economic system in which producers exchange *goods*, such as venison and corn, with one another.

In an exchange economy in which goods are swapped directly, the method of exchange is known as *barter*. Barter has drawbacks.

Suppose you have venison and want corn. You must find a person who has corn and wants venison.

You may find several people with corn who don't want venison. You may also find people who want venison but have no corn.

With none of these people can you trade. As has been aptly observed, barter is frequently characterized by a want of coincidence, rather than by a coincidence of wants.

But unlike venison or corn, which few people want all of the time, there are some goods that most people want most of the time. Gold is such a good.

So, if you can't find a person with corn who wants venison, you may be able to find a person with gold who wants venison. You trade your venison for gold. Then, since almost everybody wants gold, it's easy to find a person willing to trade corn for gold.

You trade your venison for gold, not because you want to make jewelry, but because you know that it's easy to trade gold for whatever you want. As this feature of gold becomes more known, more sellers of goods become willing to exchange their goods for gold.

Sellers build up a store of gold, which is the form in which they hold their *wealth*. They hold their wealth in gold because they know that, when they want something, it's easy for them to get the thing as long as they have gold to pay for it.

As soon as everyone begins to hold their wealth in gold, it's easier for you to sell your venison. All that you have to do is find a person who wants to buy. Presumably, they'll have some gold with which to carry out the transaction.

In the above situation, gold has acquired a new characteristic. In addition to being a *commodity* (a good that's desired for consumption), it's now also a *medium of exchange*.

Venison is no longer exchanged for corn or potatoes. It's exchanged for gold.

Corn is no longer exchanged for venison or potatoes. It's also exchanged for gold.

And so on. Gold becomes the medium through which the exchange of goods is carried on.

Here gold is called *commodity money*, since although it's used as a medium of exchange, it's also wanted for consumption in its own right. You want gold because you can buy venison and corn with it. But you also want it because it's decorative.

Many goods have been used as a medium of exchange: cattle, hides, gold, silver, tobacco, cigarettes, and candy bars, to name a few. Each has a disadvantage.

Cattle aren't divisible for small change. Tobacco deteriorates with handling. Gold is so rare that coins of low value are so small that they're hard to keep from being lost.

You hold your wealth in gold. To protect your gold, you should store it in a vault. But getting a vault isn't easy.

Sam is a goldsmith. He has lots of gold and a large vault in which to keep it.

You make an arrangement with Sam. You put your bag of gold in Sam's vault for safekeeping. Sam tags your bag, to show that it's yours, and gives you a receipt for it. When you need to buy something, you give your receipt to Sam, he gives you your gold, and off you go to the market.

You've *deposited* your gold in Sam's vault. The deposit that you've made is a *demand deposit*, because anytime that you want, you can present Sam with your receipt and demand that he give you your gold.

Other people become aware of your arrangement with Sam. Soon Sam has many bags of gold in his vault, and most people are walking around with one or more of Sam's receipts in their pockets.

At this point, Sam's vault is just a checkroom. You bring gold to Sam. He tags it and gives you a receipt. When the receipt is presented to Sam, he turns over the gold that you gave him when he issued the receipt.

But over time, Sam discovers that gold is gold. One ounce is indistinguishable from another. So Sam stops tagging gold.

When you bring gold to be deposited in Sam's vault, he just tosses it into a common pile. When you present a receipt, he weighs out the ounces called for by the receipt from his common pile and gives them to you. Once the gold in Sam's vault is mingled, his vault becomes a gold warehouse, or *central bank.*

One day, you're in a hurry to buy something from Dave. Perhaps he's just made a knife.

Dave is willing to sell his knife to you. But if you don't buy it right away, he's going to sell it to Carol.

You haven't got time to go to Sam's to get your gold. So you offer Dave your vault receipt for the knife. Dave accepts.

In this way, *paper money* is introduced. People buy and sell with vault receipts. The receipts are backed by the gold in Sam's vault.

Vault receipts now serve as the medium of exchange. When you buy corn, you pay for it in vault receipts. When you work, or sell your services, you get paid in vault receipts.

Vault receipts have none of the disadvantages of commodity money. They can be issued in all kinds of denominations. There are vault receipts for small amounts of gold to be used in minor transactions and vault receipts for large amounts to be used in major transactions. Deterioration isn't a problem since, when a receipt becomes worn, Sam exchanges a new one for it.

Vault receipts can be issued in a standard size convenient for handling. The amount of the receipt is represented by the number on it, one ounce of gold, two ounces of gold, etc.

Unlike gold, vault receipts are of insignificant value in themselves. You can't only buy venison and corn with gold, you can also make jewelry and teeth with it. Vault receipts, on the other hand, can't be eaten or worn for clothes. They have value only as a medium of exchange.

The value of a vault receipt derives from the fact that all buyers and sellers agree that the vault receipt stands for a certain amount of gold. Buyers and sellers agree in this way because they know that, when they want to, they can go to Sam, present their vault receipts, and get the amount of gold that they've agreed that the vault receipts represent. Paper money backed by a commodity is known as *fiduciary money* (O 34))

In the US, the government had the central banking job of running the gold warehouse. The gold warehouse receipts that the government issued, while the US was on the gold standard, were dollars. Anytime that you wanted, you could take a dollar to the central bank and get the specified amount of gold for it.

The US went off of the gold standard in 1933. At that time, as far as the US citizen was concerned, the correspondence between a dollar and a gold warehouse receipt disappeared.

The central bank still issues dollars. But they're no longer gold warehouse receipts. You can't exchange them for gold.

Instead, dollars are *fiat money*. They constitute a medium of exchange because the government says that they do.

The government says that all of the dollars that it issues are "legal tender for all debts, public and private". In fact, it prints this dictum right on its dollar bills. *Legal tender* is whatever the government says must be accepted in payment of debts.

We now come to the point where I'm going to deviate from the customary use of a term. I'm going to use the unmodified term, *money*, to refer to the medium of exchange provided by the government. To some extent, this is a conforming definition, in that, from time to time, what people use as a medium of exchange but isn't issued by the government is referred to as a *money substitute*.

But in general, people use the word money to refer to anything that's used as medium of exchange whether it's issued by the government or is a money substitute. In particular, when people speak of the money supply, they're referring to this undifferentiated collection of government issued money and money substitutes.

That's not how I'm going to use the term, money. When I use the term, I'm referring to just the money issued by the government. And when I talk about the *money supply*, I'm referring strictly to the money in the economy that's supplied by the government.

The disadvantages of money are that it's easy to lose and it's too negotiable. If you lose a $100 bill, you've lost the ability to buy $100 worth of goods.

If Mary finds the $100 bill that you lost, she can use it as money. No one, including you and Mary, has any way of knowing whether or not the $100 that she's using is the one that you lost. All $100 bills look the same, and one is as good as the next.

At this point, Jack comes up with an idea. He opens a money warehouse.

You bring money to Jack and deposit it in his money warehouse. Jack notes in a book how much you've deposited and gives you some blank warehouse receipts.

Then if you want to buy a knife from Dave for five dollars, you fill out a warehouse receipt to say that Jack is to pay Dave five dollars whenever he wants it, and sign the receipt. In this way, nobody can get money for the receipt, or *cash* it, but Dave.

When Dave cashes the receipt, Jack reduces by five dollars the balance of money that you have on deposit in his money warehouse. Periodically, Jack sends you a *statement* showing how many dollars of money you have left in his money warehouse.

Such blank receipts that can be filled in for any amount payable to a specified person are *checks*. A money warehouse is a *bank*. And what you have at the bank is a *checking account*.

Checks have none of the disadvantages of money. Until they're filled out, they're worthless. That is, the bank won't cash, or honor, them. So if you lose them, you've lost nothing.

Even after you fill one out to Dave, the only person to whom it's worth anything is Dave. He's the only one who can cash it. So Dave can lose the check without harm.

Moreover, if your checks are numbered and the check that Dave lost was your check number 20, you can tell the bank not to honor that check, and you can then write Dave another one. In this way, Dave gets his money, and you're protected against the possibility of Dave finding the original check and cashing two checks in payment for just one transaction.

We use the checks with which Jack supplies us as a medium of exchange. We continue to use money for small transactions. But once price becomes more than a minor matter, we resort to writing checks.

So far, nothing has really changed. True, we're using checks as a medium of exchange, rather than money alone.

But every check we write is backed by money in the bank. Consequently, even though our buying power is more a function of our ability to write checks than it's a function of the money that we have in our pockets, over all, the *buying power* in the economy is still represented by the money supply.

However, let's continue. Sometimes we take a check that we've received to the bank and cash it.

But mostly, we just deposit the checks that we've received in the bank. In this way, we replenish our checking accounts so that we can write more checks. As a consequence, few checks are ever presented to Jack with a request for money.

Perhaps Jack has $10,000 is his bank. It's unlikely that, on any one day, Jack pays out more than $200 in money. And it's possible that, on the same day, $200 or more are deposited.

Jack's depositors have the right to write checks for $10,000. These checks are used as a medium of exchange. For each dollar for which a check is written, there's a dollar of money in Jack's bank.

But on any one day, the public sees only about $200 of this money. The other $9800 of money in Jack's bank could disappear without dampening our willingness to accept checks for payment of debts. And Jack takes advantage of this fact. He does so as follows.

Suppose that Jack has just started his bank. You deposit $100 of money in it. Then Jack's deposits total $100.

Jack gives you checks, which you can fill out for a total of $100. You use these checks as a medium of exchange.

So there are liabilities on Jack's bank for $100 of money. That is, there's the possibility that Jack may have to pay out as much as $100 to cash checks that you've written.

Jack knows that just about everybody does most of their buying with checks, that these checks are deposited in checking accounts to replenish the accounts, and that few checks are ever cashed. However, some might be. Jack doesn't want to get caught short.

So Jack decides to keep $10 of your money in his bank, just in case someone wants to cash a check. This is Jack's *reserve*. It's a 10 percent reserve, since it amounts to 10 percent of his deposits. This leaves Jack $90 with which to work.

Suppose that Alice needs $90. Jack tells Alice that he'll give her $90 now if she'll return it to him a year from now with an interest payment of $6.

Alice agrees. The exchange is made. What's the effect of this loan?

The effect is to increase buying power. When you had $100 in money, it represented a certain amount of buying power. When you deposited your money in Jack's bank and received checks, $100 of money went out of circulation in the economy, checks for $100 went in, and buying power remained unchanged.

But when Jack loaned Alice $90, buying power increased. You've still got the ability to write checks for $100, which you're using as a medium of exchange, and Alice has $90, which she's also using as a medium of exchange. Buying power has increased by $90.

But this increase in buying power doesn't stop here. Suppose that George has also just started a bank and that Alice deposits the $90 that she got from Jack in George's bank.

There are now, in the economy, checks on Jack's bank for $100 and checks on George's bank for $90, and there's still no change in buying power since it went up by $90 when Jack loaned Alice $90. But if George also keeps just 10 percent of his deposits, or $9, on reserve and loans the other $81, say to Barbara, buying power increases by another $81.

And so it goes. If every bank follows a policy of keeping a 10 percent reserve and loaning out the rest of its deposits, it can be shown that, for every dollar of money deposited in the *banking system*, which is what we call the collection of banks in the economy, $10 of buying power will show up in the economy.

In other words, a 10 percent reserve policy can increase buying power by as much as 900 percent over the money deposited in the banking system. This increase consists of the money substitute, made up of bank loans, created by the 10 percent reserve banking policy.

In general, any reserve policy other than for 100 percent — that is, any *fractional reserve banking* policy — increases buying power through the creation of the money substitute of *bank credit*. It isn't necessarily true that a bank will issue bank credit to the extent allowed by its reserve policy, but it can and makes every effort to do so, since it's the interest that it earns on its loans that constitutes much of its revenue (the rest of its revenue comes from the fees that it charges for its services).

While a significant factor in buying power, bank credit is, nevertheless, only one form of credit. In general, credit is a money substitute that's used as a medium of exchange and comes into existence whenever an exchange is made on the basis of "Don't pay me now. You can owe it to me." A familiar example of credit, other than bank credit, is when you put something on your aptly named credit card. In general, *any kind of credit adds to buying power*.

The next concept with which we have to deal is *dollar velocity*. To get a start on what we mean by dollar velocity, let's begin with a single dollar that belongs to you.

Let's suppose that you buy something from Dolores for one dollar. The dollar, which used to belong to you, now belongs to Dolores. If Dolores just holds onto the dollar, the dollar represents the exercise of some amount of buying power.

But if, in turn, Dolores buys something from Ed for one dollar, the dollar passes through two pairs of hands, and what we now have is the exercise of twice as much buying power as we had before. There's still just one dollar, but its velocity (the speed at which it moves from one pair of hands to another) has doubled.

So buying power isn't just a function of the number of dollars in the economy. It's also a function of the velocity at which these dollars move through the economy. The faster that the dollars move, the greater the buying power.

In general, *buying power is the sum of the money and money substitutes in the economy, this sum being multiplied by the velocity at which the dollars, making up this sum, move through the economy.* I'm now going to invent a term and refer to this buying power as the *dollar supply.*

My term, dollar supply, is roughly equivalent to the conventional term, money supply. However, even here I've deviated. The conventional term, money supply, refers to the sum of money and money substitutes in the economy. Velocity isn't included.

It's the amount of the dollar supply that's one of the factors in determining the price of goods. The other two factors are the demand and supply of these goods.

We want the price of goods to vary with supply and demand, because that provides for the efficient allocation of goods. But we don't want prices to vary because of changes in the dollar supply, because that affects the ability of the market to accurately reflect the demand and supply of goods.

So we want to be able to control the dollar supply, so that it doesn't, by itself, influence prices. To do so, we have to be able to measure the dollar supply.

However, it's not clear how one would go about measuring the dollar supply. The reason is that no one is clear about what should and shouldn't be included when you're counting up the dollars in the dollar supply.

The inability to come up with a precise definition of the dollar supply is why there are so many definitions of what makes up the dollar supply. Let's take a look at some of these definitions.

First, there's the legal tender issued by the government. This is what I've called money. Milton Friedman calls this legal tender "high powered money", since when it enters the banking system, the fractional reserve banking policy of the banking system allows the banking system to introduce several dollars of bank credit into the economy for every dollar issued by the government.

The next narrowest definition of the dollar supply is what the Fed (the Federal Reserve Bank, our central bank), calls M1. M1 is the sum of *currency* and the dollars deposited in checking accounts. Currency is the dollars held by the public — that is, not in bank vaults but, instead, carried around in pockets and stuffed in mattresses. You can see that this definition of the dollar supply is broader than that of the money supply, since it involves bank credit as well as money.

Next comes M2. M2 is Ml plus the dollars deposited in savings accounts plus the dollars deposited in money market accounts plus the dollars invested in small denomination (less than $100,000) time deposits, such as certificates of deposit.

Ml and M2 are the most commonly used measures of the dollar supply. They're characteristically referred to as measures of the "money supply", which as I've pointed out, uses the term, money supply, differently than I'm doing here.

However, there's also M3. It's M2 plus all time deposits other than those already included in M2, such as large denomination certificates of deposit.

Charles P. Kindleberger, who spent a good bit of his life studying credit and had come to believe that it's almost infinitely expandable, reported that he was aware of as many as seven (Ml through M7) levels of the dollar supply that have been defined. His contention was that you can take this kind of definition on indefinitely.

Notice that none of these definitions of the dollar supply include the concept of dollar velocity. Some economists maintain that dollar velocity is stable — that is, that while it changes over time, the change is gradual and predictable, with the consequence that dollar velocity can be ignored when determining the dollar supply (M 323,324).

Others contend that dollar velocity is variable and unpredictable and is, therefore, a vital factor in the determination of the dollar supply (M 332). For example, if two economies have the same sum of money and money substitutes, the one in which a dollar moves through three hands in a year has a dollar supply double that of the one in which a dollar moves through just two hands a year.

Since we aren't able to identify all the sources of credit (one reason being that, when credit is needed and no existing form is available to satisfy the need, new forms of credit tend to arise) and we have no reliable way to measure dollar velocity, how can we be sure of what we're talking about when we so glibly refer to the dollar supply?

The answer is that we can't. Nevertheless, we talk, with some degree of authority, about the dollar supply, since the concept is of importance.

The *purchasing power* of a dollar is the array of all of the goods that a dollar can buy. This is the "price" or value of a dollar. If purchasing power increases, the amount of goods that a dollar will buy goes up.

The price of a dollar is what the consumer price index tries to measure. If you've exposed yourself to any of the controversy over what procedures should be used to come up with the consumer price index, then you can see that, just like the dollar supply, no one has any good idea of how to measure the purchasing power of a dollar.

As a consequence, the concept of the purchasing power of a dollar is in good company with the concept of the dollar supply. We don't know how to measure either one with any degree of preciseness, but we continue to maintain that they're useful concepts.

An increase in the consumer price index means that the price of goods has increased, which means that a dollar will buy less goods, that is, the purchasing power of a dollar has decreased.

At any particular point in time, the size of the dollar supply is immaterial to the operation of the economy. But when the size of the dollar supply changes, the change is material.

Inflation is an increase in the price of goods. Inflation can occur for a number of reasons.

One is when the demand for goods increases. Given a constant supply of goods, the increased competition for that supply brought on by the increased demand is going to push up prices.

Another reason for inflation is when the supply of goods decreases. Given a constant demand, there's going to be increased competition for the smaller supply of goods, which is going to push up prices.

A third reason for inflation is when dollar supply increases. Given constant supply and demand, there are now more dollars chasing the same amount of goods, which once more, pushes up prices. The purchasing power of the dollar has decreased.

When an increase in the dollar supply causes inflation, the lowered purchasing power benefits debtors and penalizes creditors. This is because loans are defined in terms of dollars. If between the time that a loan is made and the time that it's repaid, inflation has reduced the purchasing power of the dollar, debtors pay back to creditors less purchasing power than they borrowed.

You can see what kind of effect this situation would have. Given that an increase in the dollar supply is going to reduce the purchasing power of the dollar and that, consequently, debtors are going to pay off creditors with less purchasing power than they borrowed, creditors are going to demand an interest rate high enough to compensate them for their loss of purchasing power.

The greater the loss of purchasing power, the higher the interest rate will be. The higher the interest rate, the less likely people will be to borrow. And lowered borrowing slows the economy.

The economy will adjust to a one-time inflationary event and reach a new equilibrium. However, if the increase in the dollar supply is a continuing thing, the increasing spiral of inflation will result in serious economic dislocation.

The money supply is under the control of government. Governments don't necessarily mismanage the money supply. But it happens.

Over time, production becomes more efficient, and productivity increases. If demand remains the same and the dollar supply is held constant, then over time, prices will drop, since there will be more goods to buy with the same amount of dollars. This is *deflation*. The result of deflation is to increase the purchasing power of the dollar.

This increased purchasing power benefits creditors and penalizes debtors. If between the time that a loan is made and the time that it's repaid, deflation has increased the purchasing power of a dollar, debtors pay back to creditors more purchasing power than they borrowed.

Another negative consequence of deflation is that, in response to declining prices, people and organizations are inclined to delay purchases in anticipation of lower prices tomorrow. This depresses consumption and, in turn, production, and the economy slows down.

To avoid such a development, central banks counteract this negative effect on purchasing power of increasing productivity by increasing the dollar supply just enough to offset the price decline that would otherwise occur.

The Fed, like several other central banks, has a policy maintaining a little inflation in the economy. The reason seems to be that deflation is worse than inflation, keeping prices constant carries the risk that just a little unforeseen bad news could bump the economy into deflation, and therefore, having a little inflation in the economy gives the Fed more room to maneuver if it becomes necessary. (W 225,288)

Given that the responsibility of the central bank is to keep the value of the dollar stable, I don't see how a policy of maintaining any inflation rate can be justified. Over a number of years, even a small inflation rate will take a large chunk out of the value of the dollar.

The bank policy of fractional reserve banking allows banks to transmute many small, short-term, demand deposits into a smaller number of large, long-term investments, a process that Mervyn King, the author of *The End of Alchemy*, refers to as the alchemy of money and banking (K 104). The success of this alchemy depends on depositors not withdrawing their deposits all at the same time (K 105).

A bank, engaging in fractional reserve banking, can get into trouble if depositors, motivated by either doubt about the value of the bank's assets or a high demand for liquidity, gang up in withdrawing their deposits. Even if the bank is solvent (in the sense that it has sufficient assets to cover all of its liabilities), it may soon become illiquid, because the long-term nature of its assets makes it impossible to convert them into cash fast enough to meet the demands of depositors (K 106). The proposed solution to this *bank run* is for the central bank to function as the *lender of last resort* (K 109).

The central bank, as the lender of last resort, would loan the bank, experiencing the bank run, sufficient funds to meet its depositors' demands for cash and would continue to do so until depositor demand slacks off. Then, over time, as the bank's investments mature, it would be able to pay back the central bank. (K 109,110)

Fiat money is a prerequisite for having the central bank act as a lender of last resort. If the country is on the gold standard, the money available to supply illiquid banks with money is limited. With fiat money, the money available for bailing out banks is unlimited, since if the central bank needs more money for this purpose, all that it has to do is print it.

Sources

(J) Johnson, Simon and Kwak, James *White House Burning* (Random House 2012)

(K) King, Mervyn *The End of Alchemy* (W. W. Norton 2016)

(M) McConnell *Economics*

(O) O'Rourke, P. J. *None of My Business* (Atlantic Monthly Press 2018)

(S) Soros, George *In Defense of Open Society* (Hachette 2019)

(W) Wheelan, Charles *Naked Money* (W. W. Norton 2016)

CHAPTER EIGHT

Property

For markets to operate, the buying and selling of goods have to take place as a matter of course. For this to happen, each buyer must be assured that, when he has bought something, he then owns it — that is, that the thing becomes his *property*. He must, as a result of his purchase, come into a *clear title* to the thing. For this to happen, the seller of the thing has to have had clear title to the thing when he offered it for sale.

Buying isn't the only way to obtain *ownership* of something. The previous owner of the thing can, instead of selling it to you, give it to you as a gift.

And facilitating the exchange of goods isn't the only function of clear title. Perhaps even more important is that, if you want to borrow money and put up your property as collateral, you must be able to demonstrate clear ownership.

Ownership is sometimes given a mystical cast, as if some bond exists between the owner and the thing owned. We refer to *my* house, *my* car, and so on.

But there isn't any such tie between us and property. Ownership isn't a direct relationship between people and things. Instead, ownership inheres in the rights to things that people have. These rights are the owner's *property rights*.

An easement is an example of the fact that ownership inheres in rights rather than in things. Suppose that you own a plot of land and that you give your neighbor the right to run a gas line under a corner of your property.

While you retain most of the rights to your property, there's now a restraint on these rights. You can subsequently, as we say, "sell your property". But what you're really selling is your rights to the land, not the land itself. And these rights don't extend to the gas line cutting across the corner of your land.

The right to the gas line remains with your neighbor. Only he can sell it, typically, along with his other property rights when he sells his land.

But you no longer own the right to the gas line running across your land. You can't sell the gas line, because you have no claim to it.

When a buyer buys your property rights, he agrees that he has no rights to the gas line. He can't remove it or force its removal. This restriction is spelled out in an easement on the deed documenting his property rights.

Thus, while we generally think of property as a thing, it is, in fact, a bunch of rights related to the thing. These rights can be separated and disposed of individually. Thus, you can sell the mineral rights to your land without relinquishing your right to use the land in other ways.

In their natural state (that is, before any work has been done on them), there are only two things that can be owned: land and animals. Anything that's permanently attached to the land, such as vegetation, is part of the land. From these two things, land and animals, all other goods flow.

In the US, there is, and never has been, any unowned land. However, there are still wild animals, animals in their natural state, that wander about. If you can capture a wild animal while it's on your land, you can claim ownership of the animal.

This ownership comes about by a process called *appropriation*. By capturing the wild animal, you've, so to speak, "mixed" your labor with the natural state of the animal and established ownership.

There's little question that wild animals can be made property by appropriation. Theoretically, appropriation is how ownership of land is also first established.

A thing moves through a chain of sellers and gift givers in its passage from one owner to another. However, this chain of buying and gift receiving can't be traced back indefinitely. At the beginning of the chain, there has to have been a first owner.

The question of first ownership of land is critical, since essentially all goods ultimately derive from the land. How did this first owner come by his ownership of his land?

According to the concept of appropriation, the first owner came by his property rights to his land by mixing his labor with it. In some way, he had to improve it – he could have cultivated the land, he could have engaged in mining on it, or he could have done nothing more than build a home on it.

Once improved, the land becomes the property of the first owner and his heirs forever, provided that none of them choose to either sell it or give it away. Moreover, the ownership that they possess over the land pertains to any use to which the land can be put, regardless of whether any of them had ever before put the land to this use.

In addition, a landowner can't abandon his ownership, no matter how hard he tries. If he chooses, he can let the land lie follow, but it remains his.

In summary, land can be appropriated just once.

The concept of appropriation as the basis for first ownership was proposed by John Locke.

Well, the concept of establishing first ownership of land by appropriation is an interesting idea. But the blunt fact is that first ownership rights to land are generally established by conquest.

For example, when William the Conqueror successfully invaded England in 1066, all of England became his property by right of conquest, and he could do with it as he willed. And did he ever. It's estimated that, by 1071, when William completed the pacification of England, 99 percent of the land had moved from Saxon into Norman hands, with, of course, no compensation.

The overriding rule seems to be: If land comes into a government's hands by conquest and this government can sustain and solidify its conquest, then ownership rights are determined by this government. However, if the conquering government is unable to sustain and solidify its conquest, then the property rights existing before the conquest retain their validity.

Thus, even though, during WW II, property rights in Poland became Germany's and Russia's by right of conquest, neither could sustain and solidify its conquest. As a result, the property rights in existence before the German and Russian invasion have been given primacy in the courts of law.

Despite the shaky foundation on which property ownership ultimately rests, we would be remiss if we questioned it too closely. Property rights contribute to the stability, as well as the prosperity, of society.

As Hernando De Soto has pointed out in his book, *The Mystery of Capital,* the citizens of the poor countries of the world possess savings sufficient to remove them from poverty. For example, if the US were to raise its foreign aid to the level recommended by the United Nations, 0.7 percent of national income, it would take us 150 years to transfer, to the world's poor, resources equal to that which they already possess.

The reason that poor countries remain poor is that the property rights are defective. Houses are built on land and businesses are carried on with no record of ownership. In the communities within which these "properties" exist, there's agreement as to who owns what. But there's no official title, blessed by the government, to these property rights.

As a result, this property is what De Soto calls dead capital – it can't be used as collateral for loans. Consequently, it can't be converted into capital, which is the engine of prosperity.

And let's make no mistake about it. Property rights are rights established and enforced by the government. Without a strict rule of law with respect to property rights, we'd find ourselves in the same unenviable position occupied by the citizens of undeveloped nations.

There are a few shadowy areas on the fringes of the concept of property rights. For example, does the owner of an animal have the right to treat it cruelly? Does the owner of a wetland have the right to fill it in and build on it?

In general, we resolve such questions by having the government establish regulations that restrict behavior toward property that our values cause us to find repugnant. The remaining disputation has to do with how restrictive these regulations should be and, if the restriction results in a loss of value to the owner, what compensation from the government they're entitled to.

CHAPTER NINE

Government

It's a violent world. And in a violent world, you have to protect yourself. Trying to do it by yourself is inefficient, and what's worse, generally ineffective.

The standard solution to the problem of protection against violence has been to band together with others to provide for a common defense against other bands. To be effective in providing for this common defense, it's necessary for your band to adopt a command structure. Those with leadership roles in this command structure have the responsibility for deciding how the band is to deploy itself in its defense and arranging for training the band members in their roles in the band's defense.

But just because your band is committed and prepared to do battle if its existence is threatened by another band, it's nevertheless not the case that all confrontations between bands are decided by battle. Sometimes, the leadership of the contending bands get together and resolve the situation through negotiation. Ideally, they may even agree on arrangements that minimize the possibility of conflict in the first place.

The band's leadership not only provides for the common defense and foreign relations. It also restrains violence within the band, because violence within the band disrupts the band's unity and ability to perform.

Disputes between band members are also disruptive. Consequently, the band's governing structure investigates these disputes and resolves them.

Today, the societal functions of defense, foreign relations, policing, and adjudication are carried out by governments. And with the advent of civilization and the introduction of a market economy, it has also become necessary for governments to establish and maintain the stability of a monetary system, set standards, such as weights and measures, and establish regulations, such as rules of the road.

But governments don't restrict their activities to these fundamental governmental functions. They engage in additional activities and justify themselves with the argument that what they're doing is for the benefit of the people.

Government functions are paid for by taxation. Consequently, for all government functions other than the fundamental ones, this raises the question of whether each such function contributes to the general welfare and is, consequently, justifiably retained and supported by our taxes or, alternatively, isn't in the public interest and, consequently, should be ended with the consequent reduction in the public's tax burden.

It would be nice to have a guideline that would help in distinguishing justifiable government functions from those in which the government should refrain from engaging. The following guideline is suggested.

We have a free market economic system in which the drive for profit produces a cornucopia of goods to meet our needs. When this economic system is effective in performing this function, the government should get out of the way and let the system do its job.

But we also have vital needs that a free market system doesn't meet. For example, fire-fighting and local-roads are essential to our wellbeing but don't offer the profitmaking opportunity necessary for a free market system to provide these services.

Volunteer activity helps in these areas. But when the need becomes substantial, it becomes necessary for the government to step in and supply the goods.

It's in these areas, where the profit motive doesn't work, that government involvement is appropriate. But following the principle of letting the profit motive do its job when it's effective and involving the government when it's not isn't an easy one to follow. There are some clear-cut cases, but there are others where making the decision is more difficult. Let's first look at a case where the intervention of the government is clearly called for — childcare.

For our society to operate at peak efficiency, we want it to be peopled by citizens that are equipped to work effectively in our economic system and be responsible in their political activity. And because the purpose to life is to enjoy a rewarding one, we also want our people to be in a position to do that. For all of these reasons, seeing that people develop under optimum conditions is essential.

One requirement here is the existence of a quality school system. What it takes to put together a quality school system is subject to debate. We'll take up this topic in the chapter on education.

When it comes to providing our children with what it takes to grow into responsible, productive and emotionally mature adults, a quality school system, as difficult and expensive as it is to develop and maintain, is just a beginning. More is necessary.

Classically, the expectation has been that all of this "more" would be provided by parents (or substitute caregiver). However, time has demonstrated that, in a significant number of cases, parents don't have the wherewithal or commitment to make this provision.

A pregnant woman needs to eat a nutritionally healthy diet, refrain from smoking, drinking, and using drugs, and get proper medical care, so that she produces a healthy baby. If she isn't doing so, because she has insufficient resources or doesn't have the requisite knowledge or incentive to carry out this responsibility, then help must be provided.

From the day that a child born, they need to have a nutritionally healthy diet to support their growth. If their parents aren't able or willing to provide this diet, then alternate provisions must be made.

For the first years of a child's life, they need to be able to count unqualifiedly on the support, care and love of a caregiver 24 hours each day, so that they can develop in a healthy, constructive way. If the child's parents don't know how to provide this care, then they have to be trained, so that they can carry out these responsibilies.

Before entering the school system, a child needs to have the experience required to be able to exercise self-discipline, pay attention, and follow directions, experience typically garnered in free play with other children, often provided in preschool daycare. If a child's parents aren't in a position to provide this kind of milieu, then alternate provisions must be made.

When a child enters the school system, in order to be able to learn how to read and write, he has to be able to distinguish words, syllables and phonemes in the spoken language, and he has to be able to hold a pencil and make shapes with it. If parents are unable or unwilling to provide this preK education, once more, alternate provisions must be made.

The opportunity to make a profit by providing these essential childcare services is minimal to nonexistent. As a consequence, it's up to the government to pick up the slack.

Now, let's look at a case where the government should get out of the way and let the market do its job – health care. Health care isn't a good that the market can't supply. Health care is a classic market where multiple suppliers compete for the customer's business. The conclusion to be drawn is obvious.

If the health care market were left to operate without interference, people would pay for their health care expenses out of their own pocket. As a consequence, they'd become more informed with respect to health care choices and exercise more discretion in making these choices. In response, care providers would be encouraged to compete for the health care dollar. In such circumstance, both the doctor and the patient would value the patient visit more, which would lead to more time and attention being devoted to the visit and a higher level of compliance being given to the doctor's advice, resulting in better outcomes. (C 880,881)

In addition to improving health, a pay-it-yourself health care system would contribute to the alleviation of the fundamental problem of our current health care system, which is the continuously escalating cost of health care. It would be the opposite of what we have now, where people use health care indiscriminately, because they don't pay for it out of pocket.

It's blanket health care coverage, provided to groups where the major part of the cost of health care is paid for by a third party and where each participating individual pays the same premium for the coverage, that lies at the bottom of our ever-increasing health care costs.

Imagine walking into a supermarket, choosing what you want, and going to the checkout counter, where the clerk totals up your bill and says, "Your share is $10.52. We'll bill the rest to the government." What do you think would happen to food prices? They would skyrocket.

The same behavior is exhibited when the cost of health care to the individual treated is unreasonably low.

People, typically old and lonely, show up in the emergency room with complaints for which no physical basis can be found, because they're lonely and crave attention.

Terminally ill patients are subjected to extensive and painful treatment because the family insists that everything be done to keep the patient alive and the administration of pain modulating drugs would be fatal.

Patients demand a treatment for which there's no justification and shop around until they find a doctor who's willing to accommodate them.

People use a high cost drug when a low cost generic would be just as effective, because medical insurance won't pay for the generic but will pay for the higher priced drug.

People believe that, if it's new, it has to be better. Why trust your doctor to use a stethoscope to listen to breath sounds in your chest when you can get an X-ray? And why settle for a X-ray when you can get a CT scan? After all, the insurance is paying for it. And your doctor may be happy to accommodate you.

There's pressure to provide treatment even if there's no scientific evidence that the treatment is effective. After all, the treatment might work. And if you're suffering and the treatment is covered, why not give it a try? Once more, your doctor may be happy to accommodate you. He might even suggest or recommend the treatment.

At the slightest indication that you're not feeling tiptop, you rush off to the doctor or the emergency room to see if everything is all right.

There are existential threats, such as melanoma and heart failure, that can develop at any time. So every three months or so, you go see a specialist for an examination, just to be sure that nothing is developing.

All of these things and more happen because the people calling for the treatment don't pay for it. Instead, it's covered by group insurance, on which the bulk of the premium has already been paid, mostly by an employer or the government.

Health care insurance is primarily group coverage with a fixed fee for each person covered. This isn't true for any other type of insurance.

Insurance companies are happy to offer life, automotive, property and casualty, and liability insurance coverage on an individual basis with risk-based premium pricing. But they're leery of individual health insurance, because they're afraid of adverse selection.

It wasn't until Blue Cross and Blue Shield, nonprofit organizations, demonstrated that the problem of adverse selection could be avoided by offering services to groups on a fixed fee per individual basis that insurance companies began to get into the business.

Then, in 1942, the government passed the Stabilization Act, which limited the wage increases that firms could offer in pursuit of workers but which also allowed them to offer employee health plans as a recruiting incentive, plans the premiums for which could be considered a company expense and, therefore, a reduction in the profit on which the company had to pay taxes. Soon, an employer who didn't offer health insurance as part of an employee's compensation package was locked out of the labor market.

Beginning in 1965, Medicare provisions began to be added to this mix. And now, we have Obamacare.

Instead of encouraging the growth of a market for individual health care insurance policies and getting the benefit of its advantages, we've pushed the expansion of group health care and suffered the ever-escalating costs that come with it.

Health care is a necessity. But so are food, clothing and shelter.

We recognize that the food, clothing and shelter markets are classic markets. We let them operate without interference and, as a result, harness the incentives that classic markets generate to produce food, clothing and shelter with higher quality and in more abundance at a lower cost than is possible under any other economic system at the same time as we provide welfare for those who have difficulty accessing these markets.

We should do the same thing with respect to health care. Why should we settle for a system that produces lower quality health care in less abundance at a higher cost, when we know how to do better? And for those people who can't afford health care, there's welfare — Medicaid and other similar federal and state programs.

None of this means that health care insurance will disappear. Health care costs can be catastrophic, and the only reasonable response to this situation is insurance.

The objection to our current health care insurance industry is the poor quality of personal insurance being provided. But the reason for the poor quality product is the lack of competition that would force insurance companies to do better.

The personal health insurance market is anemic. The bulk of people have their health expenses paid by a government or employer provided plan. Imagine the vibrant market that would spring up if every individual bought his own health insurance.

Insurance companies would have to improve their product or lose out in the marketplace. The policy type that would probably dominate such a health care market would be one that covers catastrophic costs only. This is exactly the type of coverage that our current group plans don't provide.

There would be risk-based premiums. The insurance company would prefer to keep down its expenses so that it can lower its standard premiums and improve its competitive position in the insurance market. So the size of the premiums that it charges would vary with the risk involved, just as it does in the automobile liability insurance business, and for the same reason.

That leaves the case of the person who can afford catastrophic care insurance but chooses not to insure. What happens when he needs care for which he can't pay?

A true believer in freedom would say, "Too bad. The choice to not insure was freely taken. No one forced the person to do it. So he's just going to have to live with the consequences of his actions. There'll be no treatment forthcoming."

Even I think that that may be extreme. But if we provide catastrophic care treatment for someone without the proper insurance, we can't let them get away scot free just because they can't afford to pay their medical bills. That would encourage people to not provide for catastrophic health care expenses in the first place. "Why bother?" the reasoning would go, "I'm going to get the treatment anyhow."

Here's a proposal. Pass legislation that requires everyone to carry some specified minimum amount of catastrophic health care insurance.

Then, if a person in crisis is brought into an emergency room, they're treated, no questions asked. If it subsequently develops that they're unable to meet the expense because they didn't get the mandated insurance, then they're given a slap on the wrist, the expense is absorbed by the state, and the person is excused.

However, in the more usual case, where there's time for deliberation and the diagnosis is for treatment that the person can't pay for because they didn't get the mandated insurance, they'd be given a choice: Forego the treatment or accept treatment, let the government pay the fees for their treatment, and go to prison for an appropriate number of years for stealing the fees from the government.

Mandatory health insurance would solve the insurance companies' adverse selection problem. The concomitant to mandatory health insurance would be that insurance companies would be required to provide insurance to high-risk cases with a maximum cap on rates.

The government should require everyone to have health insurance and require insurance companies to cover all cases regardless of risk. It should provide welfare assistance to those who can demonstrate that they can't afford health care. And the government should insist on the creation, maintenance and use of a single, universal, comprehensive, integrated, electronic medical record system for the nation. Otherwise, the government should get out of the health care business. In the absence of Obamacare, Medicare, and employer health care plans for employees, a vibrant market for individual health insurance would grow to take their place.

Eliminating employer tax deductions for employee health care plans doesn't mean that companies may not continue to offer such plans. They may.

But it does give companies an opportunity to opt out, if that's what they'd like to do. Before Obamacare, which made employer health care plans mandatory, these plans were being phased out, even in the face of a deduction for providing such plans. If this deduction were removed, and the government didn't make such plans mandatory, they would soon disappear.

Phasing out Medicare is more complicated. Commitments made should be honored. All those currently covered, whether working or retired, should continue to be covered. But for all new entrants into the job market, Medicare should no longer be a possibility.

Obamacare would be handled in the same way as Medicare — honor commitments made but terminate the program.

It has been argued that a market solution to the need for health care won't work because health care is too complicated for individuals to be able to make intelligent decisions about. It's true that most of us are incompetent when it comes to making decisions about our health care.

But there's nothing unique about this situation. In fact, rather than being exceptional, it's our characteristic position. On most of the things on which we depend, we're ignorant. We don't know the mechanics of cars, or furnaces, or finance, etc. Consequently, when we have a problem in any of these many areas, we go to someone who knows what they're doing and get help.

It becomes clear that what's needed to survive this kind of situation isn't skill in any particular area, be it auto or furnace mechanics, the intricacies of financial markets, or health care. What's needed is skill in picking an expert.

And the essential characteristics of this skill are independent of the complexity of the help that's needed. You get references from your friends and neighbors. You research sources that rank services. In fact, when it comes to information on how to select services, there's probably more information available on hospitals and doctors than there is on most services.

Health care and health are different things. Sure, we want good health care.

But what's of vital interest to us is good health. When it comes to good health, health care is a minor contributor.

The most significant thing that can be done to promote good health is for each of us to practice preventative care — have an annual checkup, eat a nutritious diet, exercise, take care of our teeth, be conscientious about taking medicine, wash our hands, get inoculated, put on our seat belt and observe the speed limit when driving, don't smoke, don't do drugs, and don't drink to excess.

To encourage healthy behavior, an education program is necessary. An essential ingredient of such an education program would be risk based health care insurance premium pricing.

The second major factor in promoting good health is public health initiatives, such as pure water, clean air, and sewage disposal. Here the government has a clear role.

Now that we've looked at a case where involvement of the government is clearly called for (childcare) and a case where, basically, the government should get out of the way and let the market handle product production and distribution (health care), let's look at some cases where it's difficult to decide whether the government should get involved.

At present, the government is deeply involved in infrastructure. Should it be?

Take, for example, the national highway system. It was built and is maintained by the government.

But there's little question that private enterprise could have done the job, perhaps even more effectively than did the government. However, the national highway system constructed by the government provided a significant stimulus to the economy.

So, was it better for the government to step in and do the job, or should we have waited for private enterprise to shoulder the undertaking? And if we had waited, would private enterprise have taken up the challenge? It sometimes shies away from ultimately profitable enterprises because of the sizable initial investment involved.

Fundamental scientific research is another area in which private enterprise seems reluctant to take a major role, even though it's dependent on advance in this area. A lot of this essential work is carried on in research universities and is funded by the government.

Given that government is necessary, taxation to support it is inevitable. The only open question is how taxation should be administered.

We currently depend on income taxes as the major source of federal government revenue. If we're going to continue in this way, major revision of our tax code is required.

What people want isn't necessarily lower taxes. What they want is fair taxes.

If people think that their tax code is fair, the more likely it is that they'll feel a solidarity with their political system. The easier it is for taxpayers to comply with the tax code, the more likely it is that they'll believe that the code is fair.

Our income tax code is a mess. We should junk it and replace it with a broad-based, low rate code.

As far as taxation is concerned, there should be no distinction between types of income. All income, independent of source, should be subject to the same, single, progressive tax rate schedule. All deductions, credits and exclusions should be eliminated.

When interest groups inevitably begin to lobby for their particular exceptions, they should all be given the same answer, "Don't feel discriminated against. No one is getting an exception. Everyone is being treated in the same way that you are. And as a result, you'll all get the benefit of a lower tax rate."

Every time that a special situation is set up to ease the tax burden on a particular group, the tax base is narrowed, and to raise the same amount of tax revenue, the tax rate for everyone has to be increased (R 61).

An economy works best if financial decisions are based on sound business principles. When financial decisions are influenced by tax considerations, such as the ability to avoid taxes if income is earned one way rather than another, economies become distorted. (R 54,55)

A broad-based, low-rate tax code is a win-win situation. Democrats like the elimination of exclusions. And Republicans like low tax rates.

In addition to all of these benefits of a broad-based, low-rate income tax system, such a system would also greatly simplify tax payment and collection. Each year, we spend billions of hours preparing and filing our income taxes (R 5). In addition, we pay billions of dollars in fees to tax preparers and to buy tax preparation software (R 6).

In a broader context, the less that we use income taxes, which discourage innovation, to generate tax revenue and the more that we use a consumption tax, which encourages saving, the more productive our tax system will be. And a consumption tax can be made progressive, so that the more that you consume (and the less that you save), the higher the rate at which you pay the tax.

All of us have to consume, or we'd die. But with a progressive consumption tax, if you have a low income, your consumption is limited, and you pay little, or no, tax. However, if you have a high income, and you don't invest the excess over reasonable living expenses but, instead, splurge on self-indulgence, you pay through the nose.

The amount of consumption and the tax on it are easy to calculate and report. Income would be reported, as usual. Also, savings would be reported. Income less savings is consumption. And an earned income tax credit could easily be incorporated into a consumption tax.

With a consumption tax, a charitable deduction is reasonable. A charitable contribution isn't savings. But it doesn't make any sense to, therefore, conclude that it's consumption.

Another advantage of a consumption tax is that, in the event of a downturn, a temporary suspension of the consumption tax would encourage people to spend, because that's the only way to benefit from the suspension. Suspension of an income tax is less likely to stimulate spending, since many people will just save what they receive from the suspension. (F 83)

Sources

(C) Cook, Robin *Marker* (Large Print Edition, Penguin 2005)
(F) Frank, Robert H. *The Darwin Economy* (Princeton U 2011)
(R) Reid, T. R. *A Fine Mess* (Penguin Random House 2017)

CHAPTER TEN
Foreign Relations

In this chapter, we concentrate on US foreign policy. In doing so, we'll be developing principles that would apply to any large, powerful nation. At the end of the chapter, we'll look at three examples of successful foreign policy followed by smaller, less powerful nations.

Foreign policy begins at home. In terms of foreign policy, one of the most effective things that we can do to is to set a good example. This is the venerable Puritan concept of the city on the hill.

We believe in freedom and equality of opportunity. We have to behave in such a way that we exhibit our commitment to these beliefs.

However, as committed as we are to our way of life, no matter how strong the evidence is that this way of life leads to a more wholesome, rewarding existence, and regardless of how tirelessly we work to promote our ideas, there are nations and peoples who not only disagree with us but are also determined to bring us down. We fought two world wars because we were attacked without warning. We recently emerged from a 50-year struggle with Russia, which not only espoused a social, political and economic model opposed to ours but was willing to engage in any kind of action, short of outright war, to expand the spread of its life style until it circled the globe. Now, we live under the threat of attack by terrorist organizations.

In the face of such intransigence, we have no alternative but to maintain a military presence sufficient to protect ourselves. This is dangerous, since a deterrent force has the potential for metamorphosing into an aggressive one that can be used against either other nations or ourselves. Consequently, cautions are appropriate.

A deterrent force should be the minimum possible. Both fear of external force and the vested interest of career military officers and arms manufacturers tend to expand the national force beyond that required for deterrence.

All levels of command, both military and civilian, should continually be reminded that their function is deterrence, not aggression.

History seems to indicate that, to protect itself against external violence, a country must have the military power to be able to say, "You do that, and we'll clobber you," and mean it. Such a policy is expensive, but it's cheaper than war. Vegetius said, "Qui desiredat pacem, praeparet bellum" (If you want peace, prepare for war).

As a result, it behooves us to always be prepared to go to war. What might be some of the ways for us to enhance our preparedness?

First of all, we should be pessimistic. At all times, we should be looking for trouble. Early warning can sometimes provide enough time to respond effectively before a situation metastasizes.

In general, the people to look out for aren't the wicked. It's the self-righteous, such as the Jacobins, Nazis, Bolsheviks, Ayatollahs and Islamists, who tend to cause the trouble.

Given a military potential sufficient to protect ourselves against external aggression, and given that, to make this potential effective, we must, on occasion, use it, it's in our interests to have a clear guideline as to when we should engage in military action and when we should refrain.

One of the most ancient and enduring principles of international relations is the *sovereignty of nations*, the right of each nation to do as it will within its borders. With one exception, we have no right to interfere with what another nation does. The exception is when that nation becomes a clear and present danger to our vital national interests.

We don't want other nations telling us what to do within our borders. Consequently, as a matter of principle, we shouldn't interfere with the internal matters of other nations. In addition to the ethics of the matter, there are practical reasons for keeping our nose out of other people's business.

Even if we have the power to do so without fear of retaliation, interfering in another nation's domestic matters is going to be resented, not only by the nation on which we impose our will, but even more importantly, by the other members of the congress of nations. We may be powerful, but our power isn't without limits and we need the support and cooperation of the international community to most effectively look after our interests.

At worst, attempting to involve ourselves in the internal working of another nation can lead to war, and war is destabilizing. It's elusive, untamed, costly, difficult to control, fraught with surprise, and sure to give rise to unintended consequences (B 160). As Churchill said, "The statesman who yields to war fever is no longer the master of policy, but the slave of unforeseeable and uncontrollable events." (B 157)

When we go to war, the best that we're going to be able to do is win. We're then faced with what to do after the war is won.

Clausewitz said that war is "an act of violence to compel our opponent to fulfill our will." (Cl 75) Our enemy is doing something that we don't want him to do, and we go to war to stop him from doing it. Consequently, when it comes to war, the overall strategy has to be to *clear, hold and build*.

The war is the clearing operation, which is concerned with defeating the enemy and stopping him from doing what we don't want him to do.

But to see that the enemy continues to refrain from doing what we don't want him to do after the war is over, it's necessary to undertake a holding operation — garrisoning the cleared area with our or friendly troops that are charged with seeing to it that the enemy continues to behave. However, a holding operation can never be more than a short-term solution to the problem.

In the long run, holding is costly, dangerous (it fosters insurgency), and politically problematic (continued occupation ultimately comes to be seen by other nations as colonialism). The only lasting solution is to build a stable, healthy, indigenous political order that allows the local population to thrive in harmony with us, which requires a large investment in time and effort. (R 278,279)

All of which says something about how hard we should think about the long-term before we contemplate injecting ourselves into a trouble spot. Before considering war, we should define goals precisely and check the price of a clear, hold and build operation before buying (R 285).

As one of our more astute secretaries of state said, "[The US] goes not abroad, in search of monsters to destroy. She is the well-wisher to the freedom and independence of all. She is the champion and vindicator of her own. … America … well knows that by once enlisting under other banners than her own, were they even the banners of foreign independence, she would involve herself beyond the powers of extraction, in all the wars of interest and intrigue, of individual avarice, envy, and ambition, which assume the colors and usurp the standard of freedom. The fundamental maxim of her policy would insensibly change from liberty to force … She might become dictatress of the world. She would be no longer the ruler of her own spirit." (John Quincy Adams)

Since the end of the Cold War, we've departed from this foreign policy. We started to think of ourselves as the world's policeman and began involving ourselves in the affairs of other nations. As a consequence, we've engaged in an addictive pursuit of chronic crisis management all over the world (U 261,296).

Our interventions in the affairs of other countries aren't justified in terms of national interest. Instead, they're cast as a moral imperative requiring us to step in and battle evil.

This policy has damaged us, both politically and economically (U 283). Attempting to police the world requires a globe-girdling web of military bases, which entangles us in alliances that we might not otherwise find desirable, creates security issues that would otherwise not exist (U 2), justifies covert operations (U 95,98), and runs up the military budget (U 65).

In sum, the results of this new foreign policy haven't worked out well. We need to return to a noninterventionist foreign policy.

We should approach other nations as a friend who wishes them well. When disagreements appear, we should avoid provocation and escalation and try to resolve issues. Our posture should be one of conciliation, not confrontation.

One of the problems that we face today is international terrorism. The overall defense against terrorist attack is intelligence that detects and thwarts attacks before they occur and steps that deny, to terrorists, the resources that they need, such as financing. (H 166). In gathering intelligence, we need the help of other nations, and we need their cooperation in denying resources to terrorists. We can't do it by ourselves. (H 78)

It's not economically feasible for us to protect against all attacks. It would cost more than the damage that an attack would cause.

We have to confine ourselves to providing extensive security measures for hypersensitive targets (such as power and communications grids) and being satisfied with a lesser degree of security for the vastly larger number of targets available. Terrorists may take the position that, for attacks to achieve the proper fear level, they have to be against major targets, which gives us our best chance to defend ourselves.

However, if terrorists are satisfied with demonstrations, they can choose among the many lesser targets and achieve success and considerable destruction. The best that we can do in these situations is to optimize our rapid response to contain damage.

With all terrorist attacks, what we have to protect against is letting a successful attack create enough fear to cause us to reduce our commitment to our individual freedoms under the misconception that doing so will reduce the probability of such attacks. Such a reduction of our civil liberties would be self-defeating and would concede the battle to the terrorists. (H 26)

We have to be resilient. When a terrorist attack occurs, we have to clean up the mess, bounce back, and continue the life that we know is productive and rewarding. Such a response demonstrates the futility of the attack.

The only devastating attack that terrorists can carry out is the explosion of a nuclear device. That's why it's important to reduce the existence of nuclear weapons and to securely lock up both the ones that remain and all stockpiles of weapons-grade nuclear material.

It's in everyone's interest to reduce the stockpile of nuclear weapons. One of the ways that we can promote this reduction is to set an example and eliminate our own stockpile.

Nuclear weapons are ineffective as deterrents, since using them is impossible. In addition, they're unnecessary.

Modern conventional weapons are adequate for deterrence. They're lethal and accurate. And they're credible — they can be used. (B 179)

We should make it clear that terrorism doesn't pay by capturing or killing terrorists. The primary weapon here is, once more, intelligence. And that means cooperating with the intelligence agencies of other countries.

If we again experience an attack on the order of 9/11, we should respond with a blow all out of proportion to the attack. We should bomb all of the terrorist camps of which we know until they're reduced to rubble without regard to whether the particular camp was or was not involved in the attack and without consideration for collateral damage. This is in keeping with the policy articulated by General Sherman on his march through Georgia and South Carolina. "We cannot change the hearts of the people of the South," he said, "But we can make war so terrible ... that generations would pass away before they would again appeal to it."

Finland v. the Soviet Union

In October 1939, the Soviet Union made two demands on Finland. One was that the border between the Finnish province of Karelia and Russia be moved further away from Leningrad. The other was that Russia be allowed to establish a naval base on Finland's south coast. While the Finns could see how conceding to these demands would allow Russia to strengthen its defenses against invasion, they feared that making these concessions would just be the first steps in the eventual takeover of Finland by Russia, so they declined to agree with the demands. (D 69,70)

On November 30, 1939, Russia invaded Finland. Finland knew that it couldn't win the war (Russia's population was 179 million, Finland's 3,700,000. Russia had tanks and aircraft, Finland none.), but it decided to resist anyhow. This resistance was known as the Winter War. (D 71)

Surprisingly, Finland's defense, made up of things like Molotov cocktails and ski troops dressed in white uniforms, held (D 72,73). In March 1940, a peace agreement, in which Finland conceded more than the Russians had originally demanded, was signed (D 77). Russia took over all of the Finnish province of Karelia, gained the use of the Finnish port of Hanko as a naval base, and took over territory further north on the Finnish-Russian border. But the Finns had demonstrated that, if Russia wanted to take over Finland, it would be a painful and costly endeavor (D 78).

In 1941, when Germany attacked Russia, the Finns knew that remaining neutral wasn't an option – doing so would just make Finland a battleground for invading armies. So the Finns chose what they thought was the lesser of two evils – they sided with Germany. This war with Russia was known as the Continuation War. (D 79)

Finnish troops regained Karelia and drove the Russians out of Hanko. But after December 1941, nothing further happened in the Continuation War for the next three years. Finns denied that they were German allies. They called themselves co-belligerents. (D 80)

In June 1944, Russia launched a big offensive against Finland. They broke through Finland's defensive line, but the Finns then succeeded in stabilizing the front in July 1944. (D 81)

Finland then sued for peace and signed a new treaty. Russia took back Karelia and its base in Hanko, and the Finns had to agree to drive out the 20,000 Germans stationed in northern Finland, which it did at great cost – the Germans destroyed everything of value as they retreated. (D 81)

The Finns also had to agree to prosecute their "war criminals", who were defined as Finland's leaders during the wars with Russia. The Finns did so, to prevent the Russians from doing it (the Russians would probably have imposed death sentences). The leaders were given prison sentences, which they served in comfortable prisons designed for the purpose and then returned to their high ranking public positions. (D 82,83)

With the end of WW II in Europe, Finland now had to face the fact that it was a small, weak country sharing a long border with one of the two superpowers that emerged from the Second World War, a superpower that was currently drawing its neighboring European countries into its orbit. How was Finland going to avoid a similar fate? (D 85)

Finland did so by adopting a policy that was known as the Paasikivi-Kekkonen line, named after the two Finnish presidents who, for 35 years, formulated and carried out the policy (Juho Paasikivi, 1946-1956; Urho Kekkonen, 1956-1981). Finland recognized that it had to understand and constantly keep in mind Russia's point of view. It talked frequently with Russian government officials and won and maintained Russia's trust by proving that Finland would keep its word and fulfill its agreements. This required sacrificing some economic independence and some freedom to speak without restraint. (D 85)

To maintain its cordial relationships with Russia, the Finnish government and press avoided criticizing Russia. The Finnish press had nothing to say about the Soviet invasions of Hungary, Czechoslovakia and Afghanistan. A Finnish publishing house declined to publish Solzhenitsyn's novel, *Gulag Archipelago*. (D 89)

The payoff of the Paasikivi-Kekkonen line is that Russia didn't invade Finland. It didn't engineer a takeover of Finland by a Finnish Communist Party. It withdrew from Hanko. And it tolerated trade by Finland with the West. (87)

The Paasikivi-Kekkonen line has been criticized by derogatively calling it Finlandization, the expedient sacrifice of principle (D 92). That's unfair. Finland did what it had to do to survive under the circumstances in which it found itself.

In May 2022, in response to Russia's invasion of Ukraine, Finland abandoned its Paasikivi-Kekkonen line and joined NATO. It remains to be seen what the results of this step will be.

South Korea after the Koran War

In the last 40 years of the 20th century, in purchasing power terms, South Korea increased per capita income about 14 times (C 3,4). How did it do that?

During the miracle years from the 1960s through the 1980s, South Korea nurtured certain new industries, selected by the government in consultation with the private sector, through tariff protection, subsidies, and other forms of government support such as overseas marketing information provided by the state export agency, until they "grew up" enough, by absorbing new technologies and establishing effective organizations, to withstand international competition. The government owned all of the banks, so it could direct credit where it wanted the credit to go. Some projects were undertaken by state owned enterprises, the steel maker POSCO being the outstanding example. The government had absolute control over scarce foreign exchange, which was used to import vital machinery and technical know-how. Violation of foreign exchange controls carried a potential death penalty. (C 14,15)

Defying our advice and the advice of our surrogates, the IMF, the World Bank, and the WTO, South Korea didn't open its capital market to the world without restraint. Doing so would have devastated a developing nation. International capital flows are volatile and tend to come during good times, creating asset bubbles, and go during bad times, making the economic downturns even worse. (C 86)

The US and Tariffs

At one time, the US was a small, weak nation. Up to the 1920s, to protect its infant industries from foreign competition until they became powerful enough to compete on global terms, it sat behind a high tariff wall. In fact, it was Hamilton who invented the term "infant industry".

Sources

(B) Bacevich, Andrew J. *The Limits of Power*

(C) Chang, Ha-Joon *Bad Samaritans* (Bloomsbury 2008)

(Cl) Clausewitz, Carl von *On War* (Princeton U 1989)

(D) Diamond, Jared *Upheaval* (Hachette 2019)

(H) Heymann, Philip B. *Terrorism, Freedom, and Security* (MIT Press 2003)

(R) Rose, Gideon *How Wars End* (Simon & Schuster 2010)

(U) Unger, David C. *The Emergency State* (Penguin 2012)

CHAPTER ELEVEN

Education

As we've said, for our society to operate at peak efficiency, we want it peopled by citizens that are equipped to work effectively in our economic system and be responsible in their political activity. And because the purpose of life is to enjoy a rewarding one, we also want our people to be in a position to do that. For all of these reasons, providing everyone with a quality education is essential.

Curriculum

It's no longer necessary, and in a number of cases, was never appropriate, to commit a lot of information to memory.

You don't have to have the details at your fingertips. You can easily look them up. What's important is to know where to find what you need and to be able to evaluate the reliability of data and figure out what those details imply.

Tony Wagner, the author of *The Global Achievement Gap*, thinks that it's still necessary to commit the multiplication table to memory. I don't agree.

It's important to understand what multiplication is. But a calculator will do the operation for you more accurately and easily than use of the multiplication table.

However, there are essentials that do need to be memorized. For example, you need to know the alphabet and how to count.

We need to be able to speak effectively and write documents that communicate. What you need to do to develop these skills is practice, practice, practice. You don't need to know the rules of grammar. (W2 111)

A lot of what's taught in schools is determined by what colleges require for admission.

Colleges insist that applicants for admission have to have studied math up to, at least, Algebra II. So students struggle with polynomials. The probability that they're ever going to run into polynomials in their vocational or recreational activities is vanishingly remote. But frequently, we're faced with the need to understand statistics, probabilities and logic, subjects on which schools spend almost no time. (W2 296)

Colleges require exposure to a foreign language. So students contend with vocabulary and declensions.

Most of time spent on trying to learn a foreign language is wasted. For those who have a flair and interest in the subject, knowledge of a foreign language is great, and I admire, applaud and envy the skill. But for most of us, studying a foreign language demands the investment of a lot of time and effort with little payoff.

Being fluent in a foreign language is great for casual relationships, and in diplomatic matters, almost an essential. It's always convenient, and frequently useful, to be able to catch the nuances of what people are saying in their own language. But when it comes to critical communications, diplomatic or otherwise, it's more reliable to use an experienced translator than to depend on your own language skill.

Then there's finance. Almost every day, most of us manage money. How to finance big-ticket purchases is a question that frequently arises. More and more, the conversion from defined benefit to defined contribution retirement plans and IRAs places the responsibility for managing people's pension investments into their own hands. Yet schools provide little guidance in these matters. (W2 296)

Schools shy away from contention. Yet where is it more important to be able to marshal facts, draw valid conclusions, and argue persuasively?

The teacher shouldn't be expressing his own opinions, no matter how well grounded. Any effort to do so smacks of indoctrination, the polar opposite of inquiry. The job of the teacher is to ask questions and hone his students' ability to grapple with thorny issues.

What the teacher thinks isn't important. It's what the students think that counts.

Extracurricular Activities

Involvement in extracurricular activities (sports, band, orchestra, choral group, debating society, school newspaper, etc.) develops strong work habits, self-discipline, teamwork, grit, and sociability and is strongly associated with higher grade-point averages, lower dropout rates, lower truancy, higher educational aspirations, lower delinquency rates, greater self-esteem, more resilience, less risky behavior, increased probability of going to college, higher wages, and occupational attainment (P 174,175,176,179).

Teacher Performance

Education is like any other human activity — it responds to incentives (Gr 221). One of the reasons why we have difficulty with the performance of our school systems is because some of its incentives are perverse.

The quality of the teacher is a major factor in student academic achievement (Gr 61, T 159). But teachers don't get rewarded for being good at teaching and penalized for being poor at it (Gr 218).

A teacher's command of his subject, as measured by their scores on skill tests, makes a substantial positive contribution to their teaching ability. Reward for superior performance in this area? Zippo.

There's some indication that holding an advanced degree in their subject contributes to teacher effectiveness. Reward? Again, zippo.

Instead, teachers get paid for being certified, getting a masters degree in education, and accumulating years of teaching (Gr 219). There's little indication that certification has any correlation with teacher quality, and the influence of a masters degree in education is nil (Gr 63). During his first few years of teaching, a teacher's skill typically increases, but after that, the contribution of added years of experience is, at best, minimal. (Gr 66).

The best teachers consistently come from organizations such as Teach for America and TeachNOLA rather than from teacher colleges (M 178). These organizations select academic overachievers directly out of college, run them through a summer boot camp to train them in what will be expected of them, and put them in the classroom. However, after completing their two-year commitment, most of these teachers leave for a different career (M 179,180).

So while it looks like we're getting better at selecting teachers, we haven't done as well in teacher retention. The challenge now is to make teaching a more desirable job, an honorable calling, and a well-respected profession. (M 38,180)

A quality teacher is an essential. But to produce, he has to be given the autonomy to run his class in the way that he sees as effective, rather than being tied down by micromanagement and mountains of regulations on what he can and can't do (Gro 194,R 143,325,Ma 133). And the school has to back up his decisions.

Principal Performance

If we want principals to run schools that educate, then we have to give them the opportunity to manage their schools — to hire, evaluate, train and, if necessary, fire teachers, to arrange for all of the ancillary services of their schools (such as bus schedules, lunch programs, text availability, prompt response to teacher human-resource problems, and whatever else it takes to make their schools effective), and to manage their budgets (K xvii,23,163,236). When it comes to the qualifications for a principal, familiarity with education helps, but management and leadership skills are essential. (K 164)

Once empowered, principals should be held accountable for the performance of their schools as indicated by the performance of their students (K xvii). Poor student performance should call for an evaluation to determine if training and coaching can improve principal performance. If it can't or if the principal doesn't respond to such aid, he should be dismissed. An ineffective principal is a guarantee of a failing school and can't be tolerated. (K 23,164)

Fundamental to school superintendent success is his ability to select, develop and support effective principals. They're his front-line team, and he should keep in direct contact with them, so that they can keep him abreast of what's going on in their schools. There should be no bureaucracy insulating him from them. (K 184)

Other Considerations

More time for learning has to be created. (Wa 175,178,179,195) There must be adequate time for class work. But there must also be time for tutoring or whatever is necessary to meet a faltering student's needs. There must also be time for students with special interests to pursue projects under the guidance of mentors drawn from the community, industry and universities. We no longer live in an agricultural society, and children are no longer needed early in the afternoon and all summer to work on the family farm (Wa 204).

Social promotion is out. It doesn't contribute to self-esteem. If after best efforts on the part of the student, teachers and school, a student hasn't, by the end of the school year, shown mastery of the material, promoting him to the next grade is just going to make his learning conditions that much more impossible. (K xviii) Achievement, rather than social promotion, is what contributes to self-esteem (K 54).

The school must be safe and violence free, so that the students can concentrate on learning. There can be no drugs, weapons, or gang activity in the school.

Instead of picking on other students, children in a school should learn that they're part of a team dedicated to helping each other. For the benefit of both the bully and his victims, any instances of taunting, harassing, ridiculing or bullying have to dealt with immediately. (Wa 180,219)

Parental involvement is important. But first comes student performance. When parents see that the school is making a difference in their children's learning, they'll begin to support the school. (Wa 173)

Charter Schools

An alternative to the bureaucratically run public school is the charter school. The charter school is a public school, but a public school with a difference. It has greater administrative and regulatory freedom than the standard public school and, consequently, has the potential for implementing policies that result in effective teaching (Wa 192).

But the charter school, in and of itself, is no panacea. Most charter schools don't produce results significantly different from comparable standard public schools (Wa 58).

However, there are charter schools that are superior to standard public schools. Some are KIPP (Knowledge Is Power Program), YES (Youth Engaged in Service, which reflects the vision of students returning with college degrees to make a positive difference in their neighborhoods), North Star Academy in Newark (T 188), and Success Academy, Achievement First, Uncommon Schools (K xiii,230) and Harlem Children's Zone Promise Academy (P 253) in New York City.

Here are the problems that inner city public schools face. Their student body is made up of children from low-income communities and are, on average, two to three years behind in reading skills by the time that they reach fourth grade. Those who do graduate will read and do math, on average, at the level of eighth graders in high-income areas.

The fundamental problem that these children face is that there's nothing in their life to indicate that academic success will lead to success in life (Ko 9). Given these circumstances, schools in under-resourced areas that do no more than fulfill the traditional mandate of public schools (present material for the students to absorb) won't be successful in educating their students (Ko 10).

The characteristic of successful charter schools is high expectations (Wa 175,178). No child gets a watered down course of study. Every student is required to take demanding classes in the core subjects — English, math, science and history. And advanced study is always available. (Wa 217)

The fundamental principle is, "No excuses," a motto of the KIPP schools (Wa 47). There's no excuse for a principal to not run an effective school. There's no excuse for a teacher to not run an effective class. There's no excuse for a student to not perform. If a principal or a teacher is producing, not results, but excuses, then the wrong person is in the job (Wa 190).

The approach is pragmatic. Ideology isn't allowed to get in the way. The object is to get results. If that's not being done, you do "Whatever it takes", a motto of Harlem Children's Zone, to get it done (Gro 205).

If a child has a transportation problem, it has to be solved. If a child is so hungry that he can't concentrate, he has to be fed. If a child has a medical problem, it has to be addressed (Wa 196,197). Since these factors influencing education vary by locality, it's important that decision-making with respect to schools be local (Wa 100 R 61,69,70).

If a child is falling behind, he's tutored until he catches up. If a class tests poorly on a given subject, the lesson plan is adjusted and the topic is tackled again until the children get it.

If a teacher or principal is doing less than an effective job, he's coached (Gro 197). If that doesn't work, he's let go ... immediately. No waiting for the end of the school year or after a protracted hearing. Children can't afford a lousy teacher or principal. The children's needs are more important than job security. (Wa 55,56,98,99,181,194,199,218) To paraphrase Gabriela Mistral, the Chilean poet and Nobel Laureate, "To the child, you cannot say tomorrow. His name is today."

The KIPP School in the South Bronx, founded by Mike Feinberg and Dave Levin, is a successful charter school. It's a public middle school.

Enrollment is based on a lottery from those who apply. Most of the students are black or Hispanic, come from single-family homes, and qualify for free or reduced lunch. Most of its graduates get scholarships to private or parochial schools. (G1 250,251,267)

School begins at 7:25. It ends at five. There's a three-week summer school. Homework typically takes three hours.

Students wear a uniform. They have to dress neatly (e. g., no shirttails hanging out).

Discipline is in (movement between classes is quiet and done in orderly, single-file rows). When addressed, students practice SSLANT — smile, sit up, listen, ask questions, nod when spoken to, and track with your eyes. There's a lot of talk about grit and self-control. (G1 250,251,257-261)

As you may have already noted, these successful charter schools seem to live by mottos. The slogan of Rafe Esquith, the renowned Los Angeles teacher, was "Work Hard, Be Nice", which was adopted by Feinberg and Levin for KIPP (C 141). Other mottos are: Be prompt, polite and prepared. And HEART (honor, excellence, absolute determination, responsibility, teamwork).

Standardized Testing

The single most important factor in effective education is the teacher (Wa 206). In a school year, a good teacher will teach a year and a half's worth of material, at the same time that a poor teacher will cover a half-year of material.

A good teacher in a bad school is better than a bad teacher in a good school. Teacher effects are stronger than class size effects. (G2 318).

So it becomes imperative to be able to identify good teachers. Certification, number of education degrees, and years of experience have little correlation with effective teaching. And a checklist of characteristics that will distinguish between good and bad teachers has yet to be devised.

The only sure indication of good teachers is the quality of their product. A good teacher is one that produces results — consistent development of educated students. (Wa 83,84)

That's why frequent, standardized testing is important. It's the benchmark for success.

Standardized testing tells the teacher how each student is doing, so that if remedial action is necessary, it can be tailored to the difficulty. It also tells each teacher how he's doing. And the test results for the whole school keep the principal, parents, and the school superintendent up to date on how the school is doing.

Student performance is the best indicator of teacher and principal performance, and their jobs should depend on it (Wa 94,175,179,195,204). If principals know that they're going to be penalized if their schools don't perform, school performance improves. (Gr ch 10).

Standardized testing is objected to because, it's said, standardized testing results in a teaching style where students are drilled on the test material so that they'll be prepared to do well on the test. Some teachers do drill their students on the test material. They don't do it because they're good teachers. They do it because they're afraid that, if they don't, the tests will show them up for the poor teachers that they are.

Some principals do instruct their teachers to drill their students on the test material. They don't do it because they're good principals. They do it because they're afraid that the tests will show them up for the poor principals that they are.

Drilling isn't the way to teach. As Tony Wagner, the author of the book *Creating Innovators*, says, "Who wants to go through the crap of all of that rote work and memorization just to pass some dumb test?" (W1 145) I couldn't agree more.

Learning can and should be fun. After all, we're wired to learn. As people keep pointing out, when children come to school, they couldn't be more enthusiastic. But over the years, the schools beat the enthusiasm out of them.

Math is problem solving, and if presented properly should appeal to any engaged child. History is the story of mankind, the greatest story ever told, and if presented as such, should be fascinating.

English has two goals. One is to learn to express yourself, orally and in writing. That's something that everyone wants to do, and once more, if presented properly, it should be engaging.

But no grammar or vocabulary drill. Drill does nothing to improve in these areas and is deadly dull. The way to learn grammar and vocabulary is to read, read, read, and write, write, write.

The other goal of English is to savor great literature, which can't be anything but fun. But please, no "great master works", such as *David Copperfield*, or run-on poetry, such as that of Walt Whitman, which just bore children out of their gourd.

Enjoyment of literature depends on, among other things, being able to read with comprehension, which is one of the first responsibilities of a school system and, unfortunately, one that schools frequently fail to meet.

Science is somewhat different. It's about how the world works, and consequently, has an inherent interest, but it's difficult.

Here tracking is probably the way to go. Some children eat up science, and they should be put on a fast track so that they don't become bored. But for the majority, a measured, tailored approach is more appropriate.

If subjects are taught in an interesting way that appeals to students' interests, the students will learn enough (and much, much more) to pass any standardized test with flying colors without even thinking about it. The test will be a nonevent. If the teacher is doing his job of teaching his students the subject, teaching to the test is unnecessary and decidedly beside the point.

Most subjects are amenable to standardized testing. Writing is an exception.

When using standardized test results to determine student, teacher and school performance, test results shouldn't be measured against an arbitrary benchmark, because students vary. Student test results should be measured against prior performance on tests. If a student, teacher or school is starting at a low performance level but test results show that steady progress is being made, then education is occurring, which is what is being asked for. (K 203)

Sources

(B) Brill, Steven *Class Warfare* (Simon & Schuster 2011)
(C) Coyle, Daniel *The Talent Code* (Random House 2009)
(G1) Gladwell, Malcolm *Outliers* (Little Brown 2008)
(G2) Gladwell, Malcolm *What the Dog Saw* (Little Brown 2009)
(Gr) Greene, Jay P. *Education Myths* (Rowman & Littlefield 2005)
(Gro) Gross-Loh, Christine *Parenting without Borders* (Penguin 2013)
(K) Klein, Joel *Lessons of Hope* (HarperCollins 2014)
(Ko) Kopp, Wendy *A Chance to Make History* (Perseus 2011)
(M) Merrow, John *The Influence of Teachers* (Learning Matters 2011)
(P) Putnam, Robert D. *Our Kids* (Simon & Schuster 2015)
(T) Tough, Paul *How Children Succeed* (Houghton Mifflin Harcourt 2012)
(W1) Wagner, Tony *Creating Innovators* (Simon & Schuster 2012)
(W2) Wagner, Tony *The Global Achievement Gap* (Perseus 2008,2010,2014)
(Wa) – *Waiting for Superman* (Perseus 2010)

CHAPTER TWELVE
Drugs

To me, it's so obvious that drugs should be legalized that I can't understand what all of the fuss is about. Regulate the sale, sure. But make a pure, safe product available at a reasonable price. Drug addiction is a medical problem, not a criminal one.

When it comes to drugs, a common misconception is that drug users constitute an undifferentiated group. This isn't the case.

One group of drug users are conventional people who hold down responsible jobs, see to the wellbeing of their families and communities, enjoy a number of activities, and happen to have incorporated drugs into their recreational life (H -1). Given that drug use is illegal, it's almost impossible to gather statistics on these users, but it's probable that they constitute the majority of users. They pose no more of a social problem than do recreational users of alcohol.

Then there are those who are self-destructive. Such people do misuse drugs. But they don't confine themselves to drug abuse in pursuing their destruction. They also misuse alcohol and engage in reckless driving, gambling, sexual promiscuity, and not paying gambling debts. No law against drugs is likely to change this behavior.

The third class of drug users is addicts. As a problem, addition is overrated. Most drug users, independent of the drug used – alcohol, cocaine, heroin, amphetamine, what have you, don't meet the criteria required to be classified as addicted (H 11,206). This being the case, it's hard to isolate the drug as the primary cause of the addiction. Physiological disorders or environmental factors are more likely culprits. (H 12)

Addiction is life destroying, and many addicts recognize this, regret the loss of all the other aspects of their lives, and voluntarily quit.

The remaining group of addicts seems to be those who seek to avoid personal responsibility. They do this by submitting their lives to the dominance of drugs. The groups that seem to be most successful in curing these addicts are religiously based organizations. The implication is clear. The cured trade in submission to drugs for submission to Christ.

If we were to legalize drugs, we'd cut down on violence in the streets, reduce our prison population, stop destabilizing Latin American countries, and dry up a major source of terrorist financing.

The black market for drugs is the purest form of unfettered free-market capitalism. The rules are Darwinian.

With each failure to stamp out drug traffic, the authorities respond by tightening the screws. As a consequence, drug dealing becomes riskier, which results in an increase in both the cost of buying drugs and the payoff for dealing in them.

Being illegal, drug dealers have no access to the court system to resolve their differences. The alternative is violence, which results in the elimination of the more conservative players, leaving the market in the hands of barbarians who will stop at nothing. (G)

One has only to look at Mexico to see what forcing the demand for drugs into illegal channels has done to the stability of Latin American countries. If by some miracle, we were successful in driving drug production out of one country, we'd just push the industry into neighboring countries. (K)

How we can pursue our drug wars in the light of our experience with Prohibition boggles the mind. Repeal of Prohibition didn't eliminate the catastrophe of alcoholism, but it did destroy the base of black-market alcohol-supplying organizations that became so powerful that they could corrupt the police and compromise local government. It also gave the millions, who use alcohol for recreational purposes only, a product, made cheaper by legal competition, that they can use without fear of poisoning themselves and without having to break the law.

The point of legalizing drugs is that it will remove the cost of the criminal activity now associated with the underground production and distribution of drugs. In addition, with an open market, we can begin to realistically assess and take steps to reduce the use of drugs, just as we now do with respect to alcohol and tobacco use.

The most successful antidrug crusade in history was the one waged against tobacco over the thirty years following the 1980s, a campaign that avoided prohibition altogether. The tool was education, and it proved far more formidable than coercion. Temperance originally involved an extended educational effort, and alcohol consumption was on the wane when the crusaders took the fateful step of passing Prohibition.

A study in northern California from 1985 to 1987 revealed that fear of arrest was number six on the reasons for not using drugs. It seems that the real reason that most people stay away from drugs isn't criminal sanctions but common sense — concern for jobs, families and friends. (G)

The argument against drug legalization is that it will increase both drug addiction and child access to drugs. Did the repeal of Prohibition increase alcoholism? And how many beer pushers have you found lately hanging around the playground? (G)

There's also concern expressed about who's going to pay for the all of the medical and social problems of drug addicts if drug prohibition is removed. Does anyone think that, because drugs are currently prohibited, these problems don't now exist? We have to pay these costs regardless.

Sources

(G) Gray, Mike *Drug Crazy*
(H) Hart, Carl L. *Drug Use for Grown-Ups* (Penguin Random House 2021)
(K) Kissinger, Henry *Does America Need a Foreign Policy?*
(N) Napoleoni, Loretta *Modern Jihad* (Pluto 2003)

CHAPTER THIRTEEN
Financial Industry Regulation

Bubbles are a characteristic of financial markets, which are inherently unstable. Unlike classic markets for consumption and production goods (where whenever the market becomes disrupted, the forces of supply and demand push it back into price equilibrium), in financial markets, incentives are perverse.

Instead of pushing toward the center, incentives in financial markets push toward the tails. Whether the situation is good or bad, it tends to be pushed to excess. In reaction to fear, depressions are intensified. And in reaction to greed, prices continue to be bid up until the bubble bursts. Investors call this phenomenon momentum.

When a new profit opportunity in the economy opens up, it's pursued by increased buying of the real and financial goods related to the opportunity. When this increase begins, demand for these goods tends to outstrip supply. The result is a price increase.

At this point, things can continue in a rational way. Or a sense of *euphoria*, fed by *greed*, can begin to build up and encourage *overtrading*, where the real goods related to the profit opportunity are bought for resale rather than for use and the financial goods related to the opportunity are purchased in anticipation of outsized capital gains resulting from market activity rather than for purposes of accumulating income from increased productivity.

These goods are the *objects of overtrading*. Credit expands to fund and encourage the overtrading, and euphoria escalates into *mania*.

Eventually, the people involved in the overtrading start to recognize that a bubble is being created where more real goods than can be used have been purchased and more investment in financial goods has been made than can be supported by the existing economy. This stage in the life of a bubble is *distress* (H 95,99).

The bubble then bursts, and *panic* begins. The top of the market has been reached, and the price of the objects of overtrading begin to drop.

The panic then begins to feed on itself. As the price of the objects of overtrading drop, selling picks up, prices fall further, and loans are called. There's a revulsion with the objects of overtrading, people dump them as fast as they can, and they're no longer accepted as collateral for loans.

The *fear* that feeds the revulsion spreads from the overtraders to the population in general. Spending is reduced to bare necessities, which exacerbates the economic distress.

Sales fall off, inventories build up, plants close, firms fail, and unemployment spreads. Depression has arrived and continues until enough confidence in the economy is generated to dispel the fear feeding the depression.

(K)

Bubbles aren't deliberately created. Instead, they're a byproduct of the human instinct to follow the herd. (M 403)

As disastrous as bubbles can be, economies eventually recover from them.

Bubbles occur all of the time. Most are short-lived and cause only minor, local disruption. Some are more damaging. Just recently, we've had a savings and loan bubble and a junk bond bubble in the 1980s, the Long-Term Capital Management bubble and a dot-com and telecommunications bubble in the 1990s, and a residential mortgage bubble in the 2000s.

The mother of all bubbles ushered in the Great Depression of 1929. Here the object of overtrading was stock, the source of credit expansion was the call loans that banks and corporations made to allow stock to be bought on margin, and the circumstances restoring confidence was the successful prosecution of the Second World War.

In the 2008 residential housing bubble, the object of overtrading was, yes, residential housing.

In the mid 1990s, housing prices began to increase at an unusual rate. Between 1997 and 2006, the value of real estate owned by US households went from $8.8 trillion to $21.9 trillion, an increase of about $125,000 for each household. During this time, the ratio of median home prices to median household income went from about 3 to 4.6. (C 237,238)

House buying is, characteristically, leveraged. Even if you put 20 percent down on a house, you borrow to leverage your investment by a factor of four.

And as happened in the real estate bubble, when you could put down even less, the leverage was intensified. (In some cases, the banks required as little as $3000 down, which you could borrow from elsewhere, in which case equity disappears and leverage becomes infinite.)

In this way, the foundation for a bubble was created. Once prices started to go up, people were willing to buy more expensive houses, since they believed that prices would do nothing but continue to go up. Banks could issue bigger mortgages, because the value of the collateral underlying them had increased. Demand for housing grew, and that forced up prices. The vicious cycle of price expansion that characterizes bubbles had been entered. (C 241)

The mortgages being offered became more exotic and risky — adjustable rate mortgages, mortgages with balloon payments at the end, 2/28 hybrids (relatively low rates for two years, after which the rate would float up to somewhere between 10 and 15 percent (C 258)), 80/20 piggyback loans in which a first mortgage covered most of the purchase price and a second mortgage covered the rest of the purchase price and the settlement costs (F 63), interest only mortgages, optional payment mortgages (where the mortgage holder could opt to make payments that were less than the accrued interest, so that as time passed, the principle amount increased (Bl 71)). Interest only and optional payment mortgages were introduced in 2003, when they accounted for six percent of the mortgages originated. In 2004, they made up for 25 percent, and in 2005, 29 percent. (Mr 276)

The government aided and abetted in the creation of these exotic mortgages. In 1980, it passed the Depository Institutions Deregulation and Monetary Control Act, which abolished state usury caps. Two years later came the Alternative Mortgage Transaction Parity Act, which made things like adjustable rate mortgages and mortgages with balloon payments legal and preempted state laws designed to prevent both these new kinds of mortgages and prepayment penalties. (Mc 29) Both of these pieces of legislation encouraged the extension of mortgages to people with smaller and less reliable incomes (Ch 63).

During this time, due diligence also relaxed. Instead of investigating a mortgage applicant's income, loan officers relied on the applicant's credit rating. The loan officer accepted, as the applicant's income, whatever the applicant told him.

The resulting stated-income loans came to be known as liar's loans. (C 241,242) Estimates are that, in 2004 and 2005, over a third of the mortgages issued were stated-income loans. Subsequent investigation indicated that over 50 percent of stated-income loans were, in fact, liar's loans — the stated income was exaggerated. (C 244) One of the attractions of these loan practices was that they allowed people to buy more house than they could afford, thus generating a larger income for the banks (C 243).

The people who entered into many of these mortgages either didn't know what they were getting into, or believed that prices in the housing market would continue to rise and that, in a few years, they'd be able to refinance with better conditions, or planned to live in the house for only a few years and then sell and move on, or were out-and-out speculators intent on flipping the property (C 243,270).

One might consider banks engaging in such practices irresponsible, if not downright deceitful. But if bank A abstained, bank B down the street wouldn't, and then, bank A would miss out on all of that lucrative business. (C 246)

And besides, politicians wanted banks to make loans in the subprime market (C 253,254). So the vicious cycle was intensified.

In any case, banks didn't have to worry about their risky practices. They would originate the mortgage, collect their fees, and sell the mortgage to a securitization firm, and in this way, pass on the risk. Securitization has a long history.

The Federal National Mortgage Association (Fannie Mae) was created in 1938 during the Great Depression (Mr 12,13). It was an agency of the government and its role was to buy up mortgages that the Veterans Administration and the Federal Housing Administration had guaranteed, thus freeing up capital so that more government insured housing loans could be made.

In 1968, the Government National Mortgage Association (Ginnie Mae) was split off from Fannie Mae. Ginnie Mae remained a government agency and continued the role of buying up government insured mortgages.

To further free up funds for mortgages, Fannie was allowed to buy "conventional" mortgages — mortgages issued by the banking industry that conformed to strict underwriting standards (30 year mortgages with a fixed rate issued to people with good credit who put up a 20 percent down payment) and not insured by the government. It became a kind of quasi government agency. It had a vaguely defined government mandate to promote housing, but at the same time, it issued stock and became a publicly traded corporation, first offering shares to the public in 1989. (Mc 6,7,38,39,Mr 13)

At about the same time that Ginnie split off from Fannie, Congress created Freddie Mac (the Federal Home Loan Mortgage Corporation), which was designed to perform the same function for the S&L industry that Fannie was doing for the banking industry. Until 1979, Freddie was owned by the S&Ls and was overseen by the Federal Home Loan Bank Board, which regulated the S&Ls.

Freddie then joined Fannie in becoming a quasi-federal agency cum publicly traded company. In this way, Fannie and Freddie became known as government sponsored enterprises, or GSEs. (Mc 6,7)

These GSEs had an implicit government guarantee. There was no legal requirement for the government to come to the rescue of a GSE that got into financial trouble, but because the GSEs were government sponsored organizations, creditors assumed that the government stood behind them. As a result, they were able to borrow at a lower rate than was available to other borrowers.

In 1970, Ginnie Mae began gathering the mortgages that it had purchased into pools and selling shares in the pools to the public. These were pass-through securities. As the mortgage payments flowed into a pool, they'd be distributed, on a pro rata basis, to the shareholders.

A year later, Fannie Mae did the same thing with conventional mortgages and guaranteed the principal and interest — if a mortgage owner defaulted, Fannie would make the payments to the pool itself. (Mc 7,8)

Forming a pool of debt obligations, such as mortgages, and then issuing shares of the pool was known as securitization of the debt.

Soon, Fannie started using Wall Street to market its securities. Wall Street contributed the idea of dividing up the pool of mortgages into tranches, securities with varying kinds of risk designed to appeal to different classes of investors, thus making the offerings more broadly attractive.

For example, you could make available what were known as stripped securities. Here one class of investors would receive nothing but the interest payments and another class just the principal payments. (Mc 7,8)

In 1983, Larry Fink and First Boston put together the first collateralized mortgage obligation (CMO). It had three tranches, a short-term five-year debt instrument, a medium-term 12-year debt instrument, and a long-term 30-year debt instrument. The mortgages making up the pool that backed up this CMO came from Fannie Mae. (Mc 13)

In 1984, with the help of Lewis Ranieri, the government passed the Secondary Mortgage Market Enhancement Act (SMMEA). It exempted CMOs from state blue-sky laws restricting the issue of new financial instruments. (Mc 13,14)

Mortgage origination wasn't confined to banks. Independent mortgage originators, such as Countrywide and Ameriquest, also got into the act.

Unlike banks, which could draw on customer deposits to finance mortgages, the independent mortgage originators needed funds to carry on their business. This they got in the form of so-called warehouse loans made to them by investment banks, which would then buy up the mortgages, created by the independent mortgage originators, to be packaged in CMOs. (Mc 134,Mr 52,96)

The next step in the progression was the development of collateralized debt obligations (CDOs). Here a securitization organization would buy up a collection of CMO tranches, combine them into a pool, and then slice up the cash flow from the pool into payments on securities called CDOs (C 260). For any one pool, there were typically several classes, or tranches, of CDOs, each with different risk-return characteristics (C 261,262,271).

There were even CDOs-squared, where the pool was made up of tranches of CDOs.

Once a firm had originated a CDO offering, it became necessary to sell the securities to investors. Buyers of CDOs didn't do due diligence. They relied on Moody's, Standard & Poor's, and Fitch to evaluate the quality of the instruments. (C 257,262)

These credit rating agencies had been designated by the government as Nationally Recognized Statistical Rating Organizations (NRSROs). SMMEA allowed investors who weren't supposed to take much risk, such as pension funds and insurance companies, to invest in securities that the NRSROs rated highly, even if they weren't guaranteed by a GSE. (Mc 8,9,14)

These agencies were paid by the CDO originators to evaluate and rate their CDOs. The CDO originators would shop around among the agencies for their ratings.

The better the rating that an agency gave, the more likely it was that the agency would get the rating job. This created competition among the agencies to provide the highest ratings. (C 262,263) The vicious cycle was ratcheted up another notch.

Then there were credit default swaps (CDSs). CDSs are the equivalent of credit insurance.

A CDS takes on the risk that a debt obligation, such as a CDO, will lose value, in which case, the CDS will offset the loss (Lo 52). In return, the CDS receives a kind of insurance premium in the form of a share of the income stream of debt instrument. (C 280)

However, CDSs differ from traditional insurance in two ways. For one, CDSs aren't regulated, there's no obligation to build up a reserve against claims, and in fact, no reserves were accumulated (C 282).

And secondly, there's no insurable interest requirement. You can pay the income stream called for by a CDS, and if the security protected by the CDS defaults, you receive the appropriate compensation, even if you never owned the security. (C 281)

CDSs originated in 1994. On March 23, 1989, the Exxon tanker, the *Valdez*, ran aground. More than 10.5 million gallons of crude oil poured from the Valdez, congealed in the icy waters off of Alaska, and ultimately coated 1500 miles of Alaskan shoreline. (N 182,183)

In 1994, Exxon borrowed $4.8 billion from J. P. Morgan & Company in anticipation of paying a $5 billion fine for the *Valdez* spill. Morgan was required to set aside capital of $384 million to cover the risk of default on the Exxon loan. (N 183,184)

Also in 1994, Morgan's "swaps team" had gathered at the Boca Raton Resort and Club for an off-site brainstorming weekend. One of the problems that they tackled was how Morgan could avoid having to set aside the $384 million for the Exxon loan. (N 183,184)

The 25-year-old Blythe Masters came up with the idea, to which the European Bank for Reconstruction and Development (EBRD) was agreeable, for the EBRD, for an annual fee, to guarantee that, in the event of default on the Exxon loan, the EBRD would make Morgan good. It was the first CDS. (N 184.185)

According to the Bank for International Settlements, by June of 2007, there were CDSs on $42.6 trillion of debt (C 281,282). About 80 percent of these CDSs were naked — the holders of the CDSs didn't hold the underlying security (Bl 67).

Financing this boom was money pouring into CDOs from all over the world (Ch 19 Mau 102). And from November 2001 to February 2005, the Fed kept the federal funds rate below 2.5 percent (C 223), making the cost of credit relatively cheap.

The financial community not only created these new financial products, it also invested in them. Low interest rates encouraged the carry trade. A firm would borrow to buy CDOs that returned a higher rate than what it cost to borrow the money. In addition, not all CDO tranches were equally marketable, and to keep up the volume of CDOs being issued and the profits that they brought in, originators would hold onto the less marketable tranches themselves (C 273,274).

Banks, in particular, found that holding CDOs was desirable. The Basel rules, established by the Basel Committee on Banking Supervision, a group formed to establish global bank capital requirements, considered mortgage backed instruments to be less risky than commercial loans, even though, as events later demonstrated, the opposite was the case.

The riskier a bank's holdings, the more capital it had to hold. Consequently, according to the Basel rules, a bank could reduce the capital that it had to hold by preferring CDOs to commercial loans. (Mc

59,60) And the less capital a bank had to hold, the more capital it had for investment.

Banks enhanced their borrowing ability through the use of off balance sheet units known as special investment vehicles (SIVs). The Basel rules allowed for these units, subject to the requirement that the duration of their credit lines be less than year.

If a SIV met this requirement, then the bank didn't have to hold any capital against the SIV. (Mc 60) Consequently, banks would park the CDOs that they owned in a SIV, which was financed by short-term borrowing. In this way, neither the CDOs nor the short-term borrowing appeared on the bank's books, which allowed them to appear to be in better financial shape than they were, and on the basis of this appearance, they were able to enhance their borrowing.

Also augmenting the ability of large financial institutions to borrow was the idea that they were "too big to fail" — that because their failure would cause such disruption in the financial markets, the government would have no choice but to bail them out. As a result, creditors were more willing to lend to large firms than they were to small ones.

A study indicated that, before the bubble, big financial firms could borrow at a rate 78 basis points less than that available to small firms (Re 209). Because of this significant advantage, the large firms could ramp up their leverage even further together with the attendant risk.

So the party spun on. Any organization that didn't participate fell behind its competitors. As Charles Prince, the CEO of Citigroup, said, " ... as long as the music is playing you've got to get up and dance." (C 12,296)

What was happening was the construction of a tower of financial assets consisting of floor after floor of derivatives all financed by debt. The base on which the tower sat was made up of real assets — residential housing and the land on which the houses sat.

The foundation of the tower was made up of mortgages based on and deriving their value from the housing on which they were taken out. On the first floor were CMOs, deriving their value from the mortgages that backed them up.

On the second floor were CDOs, deriving their value from the CMO tranches that backed them up. Then, on the third floor, came

CDOs-squared, deriving their value from the CDO tranches that backed them up.

CDSs piggybacked on these debt instruments.

This tower of derivatives held as long as its foundation remained solid. But the foundation, was rotten. Because of mortgages with stepped up interest rates and liar loans, people became unable to meet their mortgage commitments, the foundation started to crumble, and ultimately, the tower collapsed. (Ch 238,239)

In the summer of 2006, the Case-Shiller index of housing prices peaked (Le 95), and the skin of the bubble was beginning to show strain. Between September 2007 and September 2008, house prices fell 32 percent (C 311). People found that they were "under water" – the size of their mortgage was greater than the value of their home.

Between August 2007 and October 2008, according to Realty Trac, 936,439 homes were foreclosed on (C 312). Firms began to write off bad loans and go bankrupt. (C 297)

On February 2, 2007, HSBC put out a technical note warning investors that the losses on its portfolio of mortgage-backed securities would be higher than previously anticipated (St 128). In June 2007, Bears Stearns was forced to spend $3.2 billion to bail out two of its hedge funds because of exposure to investments in subprime mortgages (H 51,65).

In July, the German bank IKB collapsed when two of its funds, Rhineland and Rhinebridge, faced a severe funding crisis (H 51). The funds had purchased long-term mortgage-backed securities with short-term debt (H 66). On August 9, 2007, BNP Paribas froze withdrawals from three of its subprime mortgage funds because of "a complete evaporation of liquidity" in the market (H 68,141).

Fearing that interbank lending would come to a halt, the world's central bankers, led by the European Central Bank's Jean-Claude Trichet, pumped billions of dollars into global financial markets. (Fr 141)

By the middle of August 2007, trading in many mortgage backed securities had come to a halt, and the lack of a market left firms holding paper, so-called toxic assets, that couldn't be traded and on which a value could no longer be placed. As a result, the solvency of firms became unknown, and to avoid extending credit to a firm that might possibly be bankrupt, banks refused to make loans. The credit crunch had begun. (C 302,303,319)

The crunch was particularly onerous when it came to short-term financing. Financial firms ran on large amounts of short-term debt.

As long as these firms could roll over this debt, there was no problem. But if their creditors decided to no longer participate in this rollover, they quickly found themselves unable to operate and faced the certainty of going bankrupt. (C 315)

On March 13, 2008, Bear Sterns was in this position. It had just $2 billion left in its cash reserves, not enough to meet the next day's obligations.

The next day, the Fed agreed to provide Bear with temporary financing, to the tune of $13 billion, and by March 16, had arranged for J. P. Morgan Chase to acquire Bear for $10 a share. (C 316 Bl 105) (A year before, Bear was selling at over $150 a share (C 315).)

As an incentive to J. P. Morgan to enter this deal, the Fed agreed to put $30 billion of Bear's assets in a stand-alone entity. Morgan would absorb the first $1 billion of any losses in the entity, with the Fed compensating Morgan for any further losses (C 319 Mc 347 T 221).

The Fed rescued Bear from bankruptcy because of the counterparty problem. If Bear reneged on its obligations, then the counterparties to which it owed these obligations wouldn't be receiving the funds that they were expecting, which would put strains on them in meeting their obligations.

If these strains forced these counterparties into bankruptcy, they, in turn, wouldn't meet their obligations, and their counterparties would be put under strain, and so on, the effects of Bear's bankruptcy cascading through the financial community. Bear had more than 5000 counterparties. (C 318,319,342)

On September 7, 2008, the government took control of Fannie Mae and Freddie Mac by putting them under conservatorship (B 77,79). Since then, the government has poured more than a hundred billion dollars into them to keep them solvent (Mc 363).

It was then Lehman Brothers' turn to become illiquid. The Fed decided to let Lehman go bankrupt, which it did on September 13, 2008. (C 324)

The same weekend in which Lehman declared bankruptcy, Merrill Lynch agreed to be acquired by Bank of America (B 111). To make this deal stand up, the government ultimately poured $45 billion into Bank of America (B 155).

Just two days after Lehman's bankruptcy, it became clear that AIG, which had sold CDSs on about $400 billion in debt, was heading toward bankruptcy. (C 325) On September 16, 2008, the Fed extended $85 billion to AIG to keep it afloat, in return for which the Fed, through the acquisition of convertible preferred stock, became the owner of 79.9 percent of AIG. (Bl 136 C 327 328 T 239) Ultimately, between the Fed and the Treasury Department, the government would pour $182 billion into AIG (B 123 Mc 358).

In total, during the bailouts of 2008, the Fed injected nearly $875 billion into the financial system (L 102).

One of Lehman's counterparties was the Reserve Primary Fund, a big money market fund and the country's oldest (T 236). It was left holding $785 million of Lehman's short-term debt, on which it was unable to collect (T 236).

On September 16, 2008, Reserve Primary informed its customers that they would no longer be able to withdraw cash from their accounts, because it didn't have enough to pay them all. Its net asset value had fallen below a dollar a share. The buck had been broken.

In the next few days, $150 billion were withdrawn from other money market funds. (C 327) On September 18, 2008, a second money market mutual fund, Putnam Prime, was forced to close (Lo 23).

On September 19, 2008, the Treasury announced that all of the existing funds in money market accounts would be guaranteed but that the guarantee wouldn't be available for any money deposited in a money market account after September 19. (Lo 229)

On September 21, 2008, Goldman Sachs and Morgan Stanley changed their status from investment banks to bank holding companies, which brought them under the regulation of the Fed, but more importantly, gave them access to the Fed's discount window for emergency short-term funds (B 130,131).

After the initial cash infusion into AIG, Ben Bernanke, the Fed's chairman, decided that he had had enough. He told Hank Paulson, the

Treasury Secretary, that what the Fed was doing wasn't its role and that the problem should be turned over to Congress to be dealt with democratically. Paulson did so, and on October 8, Congress passed the Troubled Asset Relief Program (TARP), which authorized the Treasury Department to spend up to $700 billion to deal with the problem. (C 328,329)

The fall in house prices and the increase in foreclosures forced households to cut back dramatically on consumer spending (Mi 38,40,42,45,50,51,71). During the last three months of 2008, spending on durable goods fell 22 percent on an annualized basis. GNP fell at an annualized rate of more than 6 percent.

As demand fell off, firms laid off workers. By June 2009, unemployment had reached 9.5 percent. (C 332)

Worldwide, in the Great Recession, roughly 50 million people lost their jobs. Among those who stayed employed, a quarter billion fell into the ranks of the working poor. In Africa, it's estimated that between 30 and 50 thousand children died of starvation. (G 188)

The economy has now recovered from the Great Recession of 2008. Most people are convinced that the massive intervention of the government into the economy was necessary to keep the panic from spinning out of control into a full fledged, drastic depression. I'm not so sure.

The payment system is made up of institutions, primarily banks, in which individuals and firms deposit and accumulate funds to be used in making payments in future transactions. It's the payment system that makes trade, other than barter, possible. To preserve the integrity of the payment system, it's essential that, when depositors make a deposit, they're assured that their money is safe — that anytime that they want to, they can withdraw their deposit and the funds will be there to meet the withdrawal.

Banks have to make money to stay in existence. They make some of their money by charging fees for their services. They make the rest of their money by keeping a fraction of the deposits, which they've received, in reserve, to meet any demands for deposit withdrawal, and investing the rest of the deposits in longer term securities. This is called intermediation, because the banks serve as intermediaries — it's through them that many small short-term loans (a deposit in a bank is a loan to the bank) get converted into fewer larger long-term loans.

Because of intermediation, a bank's funds are tied up in investments that are time dependent. Unlike depositors, who can withdraw their deposit any time that they want, a bank has access to the funds that it has tied up in its investments only when the investments come due at some time in the future.

Barring outside intervention, intermediation leaves banks open to the following danger. If a bank experiences an unusually large demand for deposit withdrawal all at one time, it may not have sufficient reserves to meet all of the demands. This throws the bank into bankruptcy, which ties up all of the funds still on deposit at the time of the bankruptcy.

Depositors don't want their deposits tied up in a bankrupt bank. Consequently, when it looks as if a bank may become illiquid (have insufficient reserves to meet all demands for deposit withdrawal), they rush to withdraw their deposits even if they don't need the money. This is a bank run, and it will drive any bank, no matter how solvent, into bankruptcy.

Moreover, when a run on a bank begins, it's contagious. It spreads to other banks. Ultimately, such a development can bring down the whole banking system and the payment system with it.

Consequently, the government has an unquestioned obligation to see that, no matter what, money to meet any deposit withdrawal is available (Mi 127). The government action in this situation is two-part.

If a bank that has insufficient reserves to meet all demands for deposit withdrawal is solvent (that is, it has sufficient assets to cover its liabilities), then the government advances sufficient money to the bank for it to meet all demands for deposit withdrawal. Since the bank is solvent, when enough of the bank's investments come due to return the bank to liquidity, it will pay back to the government with interest whatever money the government made available to it.

On the other hand, if the bank is insolvent, then the FDIC (Federal Deposit Insurance Corporation) steps in, depositors get their money back, and the bank's shareholders and creditors are wiped out (Mi 125,126).

It seems clear that preserving the nation's payment system didn't require the massive bailout given to the financial system. As Luigi Zingales, a professor at the University of Chicago's Booth School of Business, has pointed out, when Paulson went to Congress and argued that, if TARP wasn't passed, the world as we knew it would end, he was right to the extent that the financial world in which he lived and worked would end. But, as Zingales argued, " ... Henry Paulson's world is not the world most Americans live in — or even the world in which our economy as whole exists." (Br 261,272)

By responding to the bursting of the residential real estate bubble with a massive bailout of the financial industry, we've given weight to the idea that, if financial firms get into trouble, the government will bail them out. Given this implicit government guarantee, these firms become more willing to take risks, an inclination that seems particularly likely, given the human propensity to succumb to greed. If the risk pays off, the firms profit handsomely. And if a bet fails and threatens a firm's solvency, no problem — the government will come to the rescue.

Creditors don't want their debtors to take unnecessary risks. They want their debtors to be around when it becomes time to pay off the debt. But if the government guarantees debt, which it's increasingly doing, creditors relax their vigilance, with the result that debtors begin to entertain more risk than may be healthy. (Mo 43,47)

In addition to all of these other reasons why the financial firms shouldn't have been bailed out, the bailout violates the moral principle that people should live with the consequences of their actions. That those in the financial industry escaped these consequences, at the same time that they caused such irreparable harm to so many other, completely innocent people, justifiably fills people with disgust, throws the government into disrepute, and may have caused more harm to the fibers that hold our nation together than any damage that could have come from allowing failed financial firms to go bankrupt.

So, to channel Lenin, the question is, "What is to be done?" (C 339)

As we've already pointed out, the absolutely essential part of our financial sector is the payment system. Without it, organizations would have no checking accounts in which to accumulate funds and on which they could draw to pay salaries, wages and bills. Long-distance transfer of funds would be impossible. There'd be a significant dampening of economic activity.

If the payment system is the indispensable element of our financial system, then it makes sense to separate it from the rest of the financial system, so that it isn't exposed to the vagaries to which the rest of the financial system is subject. This is basically what Glass Steagall did when it divided the financial world into commercial banks, where most of the payment system resides, and investment banks, where riskier financial activities are carried out. It's primarily commercial banks that take deposits, manage checking accounts, and arrange for funds transfer.

The number one priority is to make it possible for commercial banks to survive a bank run. Because of deposit insurance together with the Fed acting as a lender of last resort, commercial banks are able to operate virtually without fear of a bank run (Ki 63,107).

As further insurance that the payment system remains secure, commercial banks should be required to hold a minimum amount of equity and keep leverage below a specified level (Ki 272,276). Merwyn King suggests a minimum ratio of equity to total assets of 10 percent. He points out that, a century ago, the ratio was typically 25 percent. (Ki 280)

Money market funds are unquestionably part of the payment system. Consequently, at all costs, they must be preserved.

I don't think that we have to worry about money market funds imploding. Their investment risk is minimal. And if a money market investment did go sour, the chances are good that the mutual fund company to which the money market fund belongs, such as Vanguard or Fidelity, would step in and make up the shortfall.

In any case, in the worst case, the government isn't going to let money market funds go down the tubes. At the first sign of trouble, the government will guarantee all money market fund deposits, just as it did on September 19, 2008, which will stop any run on the funds in its tracks.

Having set aside the payment system and constructing all the necessary firewalls to protect it from runs, the question then becomes: What do we do about the rest of the financial system?

One possibility is that, when a financial institution goes bankrupt, we just let the institution go, and then, all of those with an interest in the institution can go to bankruptcy court and battle over what remains of the institution's assets.

But that would be disruptive. The object is to make financial failure less frequent and, when it does occur, less disruptive.

Industrial safety experts regard complexity (being made up of many separate, interacting parts (S 368)) and tight coupling as making inevitable failures more likely to be catastrophic (Ha 216).

Applying this thinking to the financial sector would mean that investment banks, insurance companies, brokers, mutual funds, hedge funds, private equity, proprietary trading, debt securitization, and rating agencies should all be separate firms walled off from one another and doing only what is called for by their specialty, whether they're operating domestically or internationally. This would reduce systemic risk (tight coupling) and keep firms small enough to fail (less complexity).

Access to government deposit insurance and last resort lending should be restricted to commercial banks, money market funds, and whatever other institutions make up the payment system. All other financial institutions should be on their own. In particular, this means no government guarantees for debt securitizers, such as Fannie Mae and Freddie Mac.

Mutual funds, hedge funds, private equity, proprietary trading, and debt securitizers should be prohibited from issuing stock. This means that they would have to be privately funded, probably by the formation of partnerships, which would cut down on excessive risk taking.

Purchase of a CDS without owning the bond being insured should be prohibited. Buying a CDS in anticipation that the bond is going to default is similar to selling a stock short. But there's an essential difference.

Before you can short a stock, it has to be in your possession. If you don't already own it, you have to borrow it before you can short it. It's the manifestation of insurable interest in the stock world.

Accounting tricks, such as setting up SIVs, shouldn't be allowed.

Reward systems should be more long-term. Instead of awarding a trader with a large bonus when he has a good year, because it's not easy to claw back the money when he follows with a bad year, bonuses should be based on longer term, such as five years, performance. (R 164)

Rating agencies should be legally liable for the quality of the ratings that they issue (Bl 81).

Finally, any firm, that gets into so much trouble that it's unable to recover, must be allowed to fail.

More generally, the financial community should do what it's supposed to be doing (allocating resources effectively), not on awarding individuals excessive income (M 404).

With the exception of a wave of the hand at undependable contingency plans for winding down financial institutions, the 2300-page Wall Street Reform and Consumer Protection Act enacted by the government on July 21, 2010, which was designed to regulate the financial industry, (Mc 358) does none of the things that we've just listed. It didn't even resuscitate Glass Steagall.

Instead, this Dodd-Frank bill continues to favor sprawling megabanks whose complexity often brings tax advantages and are seen as better credit risks (Ha 204). The "too big to fail" problem has not only not been addressed, it has gotten bigger. (Ki 261)

Will we have another bubble? As it now stands, it's a certainty.

When? Who knows?

What will the next object of overtrading be? It's anyone's guess.

Appendix

Here's an example of how a risky investment can get a triple A rating (S 26,27). Imagine a pool of mortgages on which you're going to issue a CMO. There are five mortgages in the pool, each of which has a five percent possibility of going into default.

You set up the CMO so that it consists of five tranches, A, B, C, D, and E. If one of the five mortgages goes into default, then tranch E doesn't pay out.

If two mortgages go into default, then tranches D and E don't pay out. And so on, until it takes a default on all five mortgages for tranch A to fail to pay out.

Now, if there's no correlation between the possibility that one of the mortgages might go into default and the possibility that any of the other mortgages might also go into default (that is, if these possibilities are independent of each other, such that the reason why one mortgage might go into default is different from the reason why any of the other four mortgages might go into default), then the probability that tranch A will fail to pay out is five percent raised to the fifth power, which is one chance in 3,200,000, which certainly qualifies the tranch for a triple A rating.

But if there's perfect correlation between the possibilities of the mortgages going into default (that is, the reason why one mortgage might go into default is the same reason why the other mortgages might also go into default), then if one mortgage goes into default, it's virtually certain that the other four mortgages will also go into default. In this case, tranch A is just as risky as tranch E, or any of the other tranches. In the case of all tranches, the possibility that the tranch may not pay out is five percent, which doesn't qualify any of them for a triple A rating.

In the case of the recent residential housing bubble, the situation was characterized more by the second of the above scenarios than by the first, but the rating agencies based their ratings on the first scenario.

Sources

(B) Bartiromo, Maria *The Weekend That Changed Wall Street* (Penguin 2010)

(Bl) Blinder, Alan S. *After the Music Stopped* (Penguin 2013)

(C) Cassidy, John *How Markets Fail* (Farrar, Straus and Giroux 2009)

(Ch) Chinn, Menzie D. and Frieden, Jeffery A. *Lost Decades* (Norton 2011)

(F) Ferguson, Charles H. *Predator Nation* (Random House 2012)

(Fr) Freeland, Chrystia *Plutocrats* (Penguin 2012)

(G) Goldin, Ian and Kutarna, Chris *Age of Discovery* (G&K) (St. Martin's Press 2016)

(H) Hancock, Matthew and Zahani, Nadhim *Masters of Nothing* (Biteback Publishing 2013)

(Ha) Harford, Tim *Adapt* (Farrar, Straus and Giroux 2011)

(K) Kindleberger, Charles P. *Manias, Panics, and Crashes*

(Ki) King, Merwyn *The End of Alchemy* (W.W. Norton 2016)

(L) Leonard, Christopher *The Lords of Easy Money* (Simon & Schuster 2022)

(Le) Lewis, Michael *The Big Short* (Norton 2010)

(Lo) Lowenstein, Roger *The End of Wall Street* ({Penguin 2010)

(M) Madrick, Jeff *Age of Greed* (Knopf 2011)

(Mc) McLean, Bethany and Nocera, Joe *All the Devils Are Here* (Penguin 2010)

(Mi) Mian, Atif and Sufi, Amir *House of Debt* (U of Chicago 2014)

(Mo) Moyo, Dambisa *How the West Was Lost* (Farrar, Straus and Giroux 2011).

(Mr) Morgenson, Gretchen and Rosner, Joshua *Reckless Endangerment* (Henry Holt 2011)

(N) Nations, Scott *A History of the United States in Five Crashes* (HarperCollins 2017)

(R) Rajan, Raghram G. *Fault Lines* (Princeton U 2010)

(Re) Reich, Robert B. *Saving Capitalism* (Penguin Random House 2015)

(S) Silver, Nate *The Signal and the Noise* (Penguin 2012)

(St) Sternberg, Joseph C. *The Theft of a Decade* (Hachette 2019)

(T) Tett, Gillian *Fool's Gold* (Simon & Schuster 2009)

CHAPTER FOURTEEN
Global Warming

In their book, *Revolutions That Made the Earth*, Tim Lenton and Andrew Watson propose that, in the history of the Earth, there have been four events that have been difficult to achieve, have happened only once, and have had significant enough consequences to be considered revolutionary.

1. The genetic code (DNA)
2. Oxygenic photosynthesis (the oxygenation of the Earth) (the only revolution not involving information transmission)
3. The eukaryote cell (the basis for the development of complex, multi-cellular life)
4. Language, which decoupled information transmission from reproduction

These revolutions have caused disruption on a global scale. Oxygenation triggered climate instability that lasted tens of millions of years before the Earth established a new stable state.

The first two information transmission revolutions (DNA and the eukaryote cell) created life forms demanding greater use of energy, which in turn, dumped waste products on the Earth. These disruptions were stabilized through recycling — the waste products of one organism became the food of another and a disastrous accumulation of waste was avoided. This recycling was accomplished through blind evolution.

The language revolution has produced a civilization that's making even greater energy demands and, as a result, is once more polluting the

Earth. It was with the language revolution that we became a significant factor in the development of the Earth.

In his book, *A Farewell to Alms,* Gregory Clark presents a grand theory of economics. As he says, it's a simple theory — from 100,000 BC until 1800 there was no change in the general standard of living (C 1,371). Then the Industrial Revolution occurred. That's it.

It's not that no productivity improvements were made before the Industrial Revolution (C 9,31) There were, but population increase kept pace with increasing productivity, and there was no increase in the general standard of living.

Clark points out that, throughout history, there has been an elite that lived better than others. But this elite was small, and when he talks about the general standard of living, he's not talking about the elite. He's talking about the mass of people. (C 8)

It was with the Industrial Revolution, with the harnessing of the combustion of carbon-based fuel to generate energy, that production began to outstrip population growth and an increase in the general standard of living was experienced.

This dependence on carbon-based fuel combustion to generate energy has resulted in the creation of a number of questions. Is the Earth warming up? If it is, is it a matter of concern? And if it's of concern, what's causing it and is what's causing it anything over which we have any control?

So, is the Earth warming up? Not everyone thinks so. But most do. According to the Intergovernmental Panel on Climate Change (IPCC), warming of the climate system is unequivocal (Ta 721).

So, will the warming of the Earth create problems for us? Here are some of the things that will happen if the world heats up.

1. The sea level will rise (F 181). Sea ice, similar to what covers the Arctic Ocean in the winter, isn't a problem. It's already floating, and if it melts, the sea level will remain the same. It's the massive ice sheets that cover land that are the threat. When these ice sheets melt or when icebergs break off from the glaciers, sea level rises. The result will be significant damage to port cities, on which much of civilization depends.

2. The world will become more tropical, which will bring with it the spread of tropical diseases (such as malaria, ebola, elephantiasis, schistosomiasis (infestation by blood flukes), leprosy, dengue fever), rampant intestinal parasites, poisonous spiders and centipedes, and new and vicious kinds of ants (W 176,188).

3. The oceans will warm up. When water heats up, it expands, which contributes to a rising sea level. But more importantly, warming oceans will result in more volatile weather — there will be more intense tropical storms (hurricanes and typhoons), more frequent flooding, dry areas will become drier, and drought will occur, all of which could compromise agriculture as well as causing other destruction (G, Ta 732).

4. Because of drought and flooding, billions of people will find that their living conditions are no longer viable (D 119,120). The result will be mass migration. These billions will want to relocate to where conditions are still viable. Those already living in these habitats aren't going to want more people moving in. Conflict will be inevitable.

5. Increases in temperature results in an increase in violence. Riots become more frequent. (D 109,110) This is going to make conflict caused by migration to be particularly ugly.

So perhaps we can agree that global warming would be a problem. In fact, I doubt that I even have to press it. As near as I can tell, almost everyone agrees that global warming is a threat.

So if the world is warming up and it's a problem, the third question is: What's causing this warming and what can we do about it?

Now we begin to get a difference of opinion. First, let's look at some things on which people agree.

The Earth gets its heat from the Sun, mostly in the form of visual light rays. In conformance with the second law of thermodynamics, what heat the Earth absorbs it radiates back into the atmosphere. But this radiation is in the form of infrared rays. (Go)

There are gases, called greenhouse gases, in the atmosphere that allow the visual light from the Sun to pass unobstructed to the Earth. But these greenhouse gases reflect part of the Earth's infrared radiation back onto the Earth.

It's this reflection that keeps the Earth warm. If it weren't for this greenhouse effect, the Earth's temperature would be about zero degrees Fahrenheit, all the water on the Earth would freeze, and the Earth would turn into a giant snowball. (Go)

The most common greenhouse "gas" is water vapor. The warmer the Earth is, the more water evaporates and the more vapor the atmosphere can hold. The amount of water vapor in the air can be as much as four percent (Ta 711).

The second most common greenhouse gas is CO_2. Once in the atmosphere, CO_2 can stay there for a long while without breaking down. Its half-life has been estimated to be about 30 years (S 392).

The third most common greenhouse gas is methane. Methane is 21 times more efficient at trapping heat than CO_2, but it breaks down quickly.

The fourth most common greenhouse gas is nitrous oxide. The life span of nitrous oxide is about 150 years (Ta 724).

There then follows a host of other chemical gases, many containing chlorine and fluorine. Many of these gases are more efficient at trapping heat than CO_2. Some are tens of thousands times more efficient. But they're rare.

Natural processes send more than 700 billion tons of CO_2 into the atmosphere every year. Without our contribution, there has been an equilibrium, natural processes removing CO_2 from the atmosphere at the same rate as they add it. The carbon-based fuel that we burn adds a fraction more to the amount of CO_2 sent into the atmosphere, but it's enough to upset the balance.

Now, each year, more and more CO_2 accumulates in the atmosphere. (Cl 54) There's now more CO_2 in the air than there has been for at least 650,000 years (Cl 82).

There's a 1500 year cycle to the Earth's temperature, where the temperature varies about 4 degrees Centigrade from peak to trough (Si v,xv). Ice cores and seabed sediments testify to this 1500-year cycle for the past 900,000 years (Si xii,6,29,128). The cycle is linked to small changes in the Sun's irradiance (Si 2), which is from where the solar wind comes.

The more cosmic rays enter the earth's atmosphere, the more they ionize the air. The ionized air seeds the growth of low lying clouds, which tend to reflect the Sun's light rays back away from the Earth, and there's a cooling trend.

When the solar wind increases, it creates more of a shield around the Earth against cosmic rays, and as a result, fewer low lying clouds are formed and the Earth's temperature increases. In contrast, when the solar wind abates, cooling occurs. (Si 192,193,194)

The changes in the Sun's irradiance follow a 1500-year cycle (Si 191), which is why the Earth's climate cycles every 1500 years. And there's little that we can do about it (Si 233).

And now the contention begins.

The minority opinion is that, within the context of this 1500 year temperature cycle, the amount of CO_2 in the air is irrelevant. In addition, each added molecule of CO_2 in the air has a reduced ability to trap heat. Therefore, as the CO_2 level increases, the increasing effectiveness of the heat trap tails off. (Si 36)

Historically, warmer weather has moved in tandem with rising CO_2 levels in the air, but the rise in CO_2 lagged the warmer weather by about 800 years. This is because, as ocean temperature rises, the ocean can hold less and less CO_2, so more of it is released into the air. (Si 11,37)

The majority opinion disagrees. It maintains that global warming is the result of the human induced buildup of greenhouse gases in the atmosphere and that, the greater the buildup, the more the Earth will warm. An IPCC report puts the probability of the recent increase in global temperature being due to human-generated greenhouse gas concentrations at between 90 and 99 percent (Ta 723).

The present CO_2 level in the atmosphere is about 30 percent higher than its highest level in the past 650,000 years. The rapid increase in atmospheric CO_2 since the onset of industrialization is obvious. The annual rate at which atmospheric CO_2 concentrations are growing has been increasing for the past several decades. (Ta 722) The increasing concentration of methane in the atmosphere has been in step with the increase in population (Ta 724). The increase in nitrous oxide results from the increased use of nitrogen fertilizer (Ta 724).

143

If you take into consideration how common a greenhouse gas is, how efficient it is at containing heat, how long it lasts, and what control we have over it, then if we want to contain global warming, it's clear that we should be focusing on CO_2 emissions (Cl 33-36).

So, here we are, in the classic layman's position. For our information, we depend on experts. And when the experts disagree, what are we to do?

In such situations, the standard approach is to suspend judgment and wait for the experts to sort it out. But in the case of global warming, if the majority experts are right, then we're facing a growing, significant problem that, if nothing is done, will create a situation where what would at one time have been an effective countermeasure is no longer adequate. Climate-induced environmental changes can't be reversed quickly (Ta 735).

What others would do in this case, I don't know. But as for me, I think that we have no choice but to go with the majority opinion.

So, to summarize: Global warming exists, it's a problem, the primary culprit is the amount of CO_2 in the atmosphere, and it's within the realm of possibility for us to do something about it. So:

Global warming is ... well ... a global problem. That means that it requires a global solution.

There's no global government. That means that the problem of global warming has to be solved through the cooperative efforts of the world's nations.

How this cooperation will come about I haven't the foggiest. For myself, I find solace in the belief that, if something has to be done, then sooner or later, it will be done.

If we could agree on a program for addressing the global warming problem, it might constitute a first step toward an international solution to the problem, because we could then enter into what would be, hopefully, a constructive discussion on how to implement the agreed on program.

To the extent possible, we have to abandon the use of carbon-based fuel.

We run our submarines with atomic power. The transfer of this technology to all marine craft should be straightforward. I'll leave all other direct applications of atomic power to the determination of those who know more about the subject than I.

In any case, I suspect that there are many areas where we need power and the direct use of atomic power is impractical. Heating buildings, powering manufacturing plants, and running cars and trucks spring to mind. In all of these cases, we should plan to rely on electricity. From where is all of this electricity to come?

It can't come from the coal, oil and gas fired power plants that we currently have, because they're CO_2 producers. They have to be phased out.

Renewables (hydro, wind and solar) have caught the popular imagination as possible power generators.

Hydro is a nonstarter. Most of it is generated by building dams, which is environmentally undesirable (Y 714).

A disadvantage of electricity as a source of power is that there's no way to store it in volume. Since to run our plants, commercial facilities, residences, and cars, we need electricity to be available 24/7, this means that we must have the ability to constantly generate electricity. In other words, our electricity generating facilities must be sustainable.

Wind and solar power electricity generation are environmentally friendly. But they're not sustainable. You can't run a windmill when there's no wind or collect sunlight when the sun isn't shining. (Y 585,589, Sm 25).

At some point, nuclear fusion may become a power source, but it's unlikely. Nuclear fusion is what goes on inside the Sun or any other star, and controlling it is a formidable task. As has been said, nuclear fusion may be the energy of the future and probably always will be. Nevertheless, people are investigating the possibility of generating electricity through the use of nuclear fusion. In any case, it's not something that we can count on today.

So, for the present, that leaves nuclear fission.

People have three concerns with nuclear fission power generation: Nuclear plant breakdown can be dangerous, disposal of nuclear waste is thought to be a problem, and nuclear power is expensive.

The atomic power industry is intensely interested in safety. It does everything that it can to see that accidents don't happen.

The atomic power industry actively pursues technology development to make atomic energy plants as safe as possible. And continuous equipment maintenance is practiced.

When it comes to breakdown, the atomic power industry is like the airline industry. When a crisis occurs, instant and competent action is required, but there's little opportunity to practice in real life situations.

Borrowing the practice of the airlines industry, an atomic energy plant has a simulation room that duplicates the plant's control center and where all kinds of complications in plant operation can be simulated. Every few weeks, all of the operators in the real control center are required to practice handling emergencies in the simulation room, the same way that pilots practice handling emergencies in flight simulators. (T)

Atomic energy generation apes the airlines industry in another way. When an accident occurs, it's investigated intensively to establish what has to be done to prevent similar accidents from happening in the future.

The second concern that people have about nuclear fission is how to go about sequestering the atomic waste produced. The atomic power industry pursues technology to minimize nuclear waste. Sequestering it shouldn't be a major problem.

The final concern with nuclear power generation is its cost. In evaluating the cost of nuclear power generation, we should consider the cost of continuing to generate power through the use of plants run with carbon based fuel.

In conclusion, we should be aggressively implementing the use of nuclear fission to generate electricity.

If we want to wean ourselves away from carbon-based fuel, we could either tax carbon when it comes out of the ground or institute a cap and trade program. Either would confine the use of carbon-based fuel to the most extreme situations where all of the other alternatives are either technologically unattainable or prohibitively expensive. And if the program originally instituted doesn't sufficiently reduce the use of carbon-based fuel, then all that's necessary is to ratchet up the program.

To reduce energy use, we should be frugal — use less of everything, because almost everything involves the use of energy. We have only one Earth, and ultimately, its resources are limited. We Westerners are currently too profligate, and at the moment, we're just encouraging the rest of the world to emulate us.

Sources

(C) Clark, Gregory *A Farewell to Alms* (Princeton U 2007)

(Cl) *Global Weirdness* by Climate Central, a nonprofit, nonpartisan science and journalism organization (Random House 2012)

(D) Dunn, Rob *A Natural History of the Future* (Hachette 2021)

(F) Flannery, Tim *The Weather Makers* (Atlantic Monthly 2005)

(G) Private communication with Mark D. Gildersleeve, president of WSI, a weather service firm, on 12/7/12

(Go) Goodstein, David *Out of Gas* (Norton 2004)

(L) Lenton, Tim and Watson, Andrew *Revolutions That Made the Earth* (Oxford U 2011)

(M) Morris, Ian *Why the West Rules — For Now* (Farrar, Straus and Giroux 2010)

(O) Owen, David *Conundrum* (Penguin 2011)

(P) Pinker, Steven *Enlightenment Now* (Penguin Random House 2018)

(S) Silver, Nate *The Signal and the Noise* (Penguin 2012)

(Si) Singer, S. Fred and Avery, Dennis T. *Unstoppable Global Warming* (Rowman & Littlefield 2007)

(Sm) Smil, Vaclav *How the World Really Works* (Penguin Random House 2022)

(T) Talk given by Michael Twomey, an officer of Entergy, which manages Indian Point, among other nuclear facilities, to the Darien CT Senior Men's Association on 3/28/2012

(Ta) Tarbuck, Edward J. and Lutgens, Frederick K. *Earth* (Pearson 2014)

(W) Ward, Peter D. *Under a Green Sky* (Smithsonian 2007)

(Y) Yergin, Daniel *The Quest* (Penguin 2011)

CHAPTER FIFTEEN
Income Inequality

The conclusion that most thinkers, from Aristotle on, have reached with respect to income inequality is that it's inevitable. There will always be a well off elite and a mass of have nots. (Si 8,22)

Unless contained in some way, this imbalance will, ultimately lead to one of two equally undesirable situations (Si 8). Either the elite will consolidate power and form an oligarchy that will oppress the masses, or a demagogue will arise among the masses, lead them to an overthrow of the elite, and establish a tyranny. (Si 18,22,187,238,239).

The classic response to this situation was adoption of what Ganesh Sitaraman, the author of *The Crisis of the Middle-Class Constitution*, calls a class warfare constitution (Si 23), where the two economic classes are built directly into the structure of the government (Si 8). Each class then has a stake in the government and serves as a check on the other (Si 8). Thus, the Roman government had a patrician Senate and plebian Tribunes (Si 23,36). And the English established a House of Lords and a House of Commons (Si 33,34).

However, there was an alternative line of thought. If a polity had a middle class, made up of people who were economically well enough off to support themselves and their families but not well enough off to support their heirs and their families (Si 13), and if this middle class was large enough to hold the balance of power over both the elite and the less well-off, then a republic would be possible (Si 8), because the middle class wouldn't be tempted by the urges of either the affluent or the less well-off and, consequently, wouldn't take extreme positions, would mediate between the two extremes, and would govern wisely (Si 23,51,52,57,113,146). Such a polity would have a *middle-class constitution* (Si 13).

James Harrington (born 1611) contributed to the idea of a middle-class constitution (Si 53). He observed that, for a large middle class to exist, there had to be wide degree of income equality (Si 54,58,164). When Harrington was writing, the economy was predominantly agricultural and income was almost totally a function of land ownership. Consequently, if there were to be a wide degree of income equality, there also had to be a wide degree of land ownership. (Si 113)

At the time that our Constitution was written, the economy in the US was primarily agricultural and property ownership was widespread. In addition, the frontier was open, and people were free to move west and settle on unclaimed land. (Si 4) The founders were familiar with Harrington's work, and what they developed was a middle-class constitution (Si 23,275,302).

Throughout its development, the US has been faced with two challenges to income equality. One is the challenge of inclusion – who belongs to the polity? In the beginning, slaves, minorities, Indians and women were excluded, and the battle has been to widen the borders of the polity and bring in these excluded people. (Si 13)

The other challenge was to maintain income equality in the polity. Over time, the frontier closed, and the availability of free land disappeared.

And with industrialization, the nature of income changed. No longer did it derive primarily from land ownership. It came more from employment. The distinction between employer and employee formed the basis for increasing income inequality. Even Tocqueville recognized this. (Si 5,114,138,139)

If we're to keep our middle-class constitution, then the overriding goal has to be to see that the middle class remains dominant (Si 284). And to achieve this goal, there has to be a relatively equal income distribution (Si 285).

At present, there's a significant degree of income inequality. One cause of income inequality is the unjustifiably inordinate pay awarded to corporate bigwigs. Many CEOs make more in a single workday than it takes the average worker a year to accumulate. Excessive pay should be taxed heavily, approaching 100 percent.

As Thomas Piketty points out in his book *Capital,* the insidious cause of economic inequality is that, unlike most, the well-off invest. As a result, the wealth that our economy throws off flows to the well-off, they become progressively better off while the economic condition of the rest of us stagnates, and the extent of income inequality continues to grow.

It isn't fair that the wealth of our economy should flow disproportionately to the well-off. We all contribute to our economy, it belongs to us all, and we should all share in its wealth.

My unrealistic solution to this problem is to have people invest in the nation by, yes, buying stocks.

This solution is unrealistic for two reasons. First, many people don't have the commitment or ability to save so that they can build up funds to invest. Second, even if they were supplied with the needed funds, the bulk of people still wouldn't get the benefit of investing, because most of them are, to put it bluntly, lousy money managers. (Nevertheless, in the last chapter of this book, I describe a technique for saving and investing.)

If we're to solve our income inequality problem, some sort of program that's the equivalent of what I'm proposing has to be put into place. A possible equivalent would be to adopt a system where the government provides everyone over, say, 18, from the homeless person on the street to Bill Gates and Warren Buffett, with a modest but significant income. Such a program has come to be known as a *universal basic income* (UBI). The UBI could be thought of as the dividend that each of us receives from the productivity of our economic system.

A UBI would establish a dominant, secure middle class interested in what's best for the welfare of the nation. And anyone who wants to supplement this basic income, is free to do so (R 215).

A UBI has attractive features. It's universal, unconditional, inclusive and simple (L 11).

But a UBI raises questions. One is: Who is this everybody who's going to get a UBI? Certainly, all citizens. How about the foreign born who are permanent residents? Probably, although there would be resistance to the idea. (L 178)

Another question is how to pay for a UBI. The cost of a reasonably sized UBI would be significant, running to the trillions of dollars (L 8,185). To meet this cost, a way has to be found to see that a sufficient portion of the proceeds, from the continually increasing productivity of our economy, flows to the government rather than to people in high income brackets, so that providing each citizen with a UBI can be funded (R 216).

Some of the wealth flowing to stockholders has to be redirected to the government. A tax on dividends would be a start. But by itself, it wouldn't work. Corporations would just stop paying dividends. In some way, capital gains have to be factored into the equation.

Once a UBI has been established, it could be increased incrementally at the same time as features of our welfare system, such as food stamps and rent subsidies, are discontinued. Ultimately, we could start thinking about phasing out social security and replacing it with an augmented UBI.

Other steps necessary to maintain a middle class majority are as follows.

Most important for maintaining a democratic and productive social system is the availability of high quality, affordable education for everyone (Si 286).

Utility regulation, such as that in place for electric service, is a good idea. Certainly, common carrier regulation is sound. The public has to have equal access to communication. The current battle here is to preserve net neutrality on the Internet. (Si 290,291)

Corporations have to take a longer term orientation to their businesses. The biggest barrier here seems to be the outsized income, based on short-term profit, of corporation executives. (Si 291)

We need more participation in the electoral system. Australia seems to have a good idea here. Every Australian has to submit a ballot. They don't have to vote for anyone, but they do have to go through the procedure of submitting a ballot. (Si 299)

Finally, there's the question of family dynasties (Si 285). Here the recommendation is to use estate taxes to disable the passing of wealth from one generation to the next.

To the extent that such a tax policy forces the wealthy to give their wealth to charity and to set up foundations, I suppose that it's a good thing. A lot of the wealthy do that in any case.

I'm hesitant to adopt a government policy that prevents a person from doing what he wants to with the money that he has earned. And I'm not sure that wealthy heirs are such bad things. Either they just dissipate the wealth, which is a waste but doesn't do much harm, or they're responsible heirs who use their financial independence to further good causes.

Sources

(L) Lowrey, Annie *Give People Money* (Penguin Random House 2018)

(R) Reich, Robert B. *Saving Capitalism* (Penguin Random House 2015)

(S) Sandel, Michael J. *Justice* (Farrar, Straus and Giroux 2009)

(Si) Sitaraman, Ganesh *The Crisis of the Middle-Class Constitution* (Alfred A. Knopf 2017)

CHAPTER SIXTEEN

Representative Government

We're committed to representative government, one in which one person's vote carries the same weight as every other person's. That's not what we have.

Our nation began to form when the 13 independent English colonies in America banded together in a loose confederation to rebel against English rule. On September 3, 1783, the Treaty of Paris granted the colonies their independence.

Between that time and 1787, under the Articles of Confederation, the colonies, who now thought of themselves as independent states, began to grow away from one another. In particular, they set up tariff barriers and taxed each other's trade.

The men who had struggled for American independence viewed these developments with misgivings and abhorred the drift toward "anarchy and confusion". Sentiment for overhauling the national government began to grow.

This urge for a stronger national government was given added impulse by Shay's Rebellion, and in the early summer of 1787, a convention to strengthen the Articles of Confederation began its deliberations. The delegates were the pick of the revolutionary leadership, molded by their service in the army, Congress, state assemblies, and diplomatic posts and recognized that what they came up with must fit both the American experience with self-government and the hopes of the American people for the future.

The delegates soon agreed that amending the Articles wasn't going to do the job and set about developing a constitution.

The delegates decided that the legislative branch of the government should be made up of two chambers, a House of Representatives and a Senate, because that's what they were used to in Parliament and their own state governments. However, a difficulty then arose.

The large states maintained that, to be representative of the people, both houses should be constituted so that each member was elected by residents of a district of approximately the same population as every other district. The small states were willing to yield some of the uniform treatment that they had been accorded under the Articles, but they were adamant that some recognition be given to their interests as states.

Through June and the first half of July the controversy continued, until the delegates began to fear that agreement would never be reached. Ultimately, a compromise was worked out: The House would embody proportional representation of the people while the Senate would allow each state an equal vote.

As it turned out, the problem that the compromise addressed has never developed. The nation has been split on issues, but the large and small states have never faced off against each other.

However, at the time, the concern seemed real, and the compromise allowed the convention to move forward in the framing of the Constitution. Nevertheless, as a result, representative government was compromised.

The delegates agreed that an elected president should head the executive branch of the government. The problem was in deciding how the president would be elected.

Everyone agreed that, no matter how the election was carried out, Washington was going to be the first president. But after his administration, it was felt that there would be a lack of people with his national recognition and that, because of the difficulty of communicating over distances, there would be a problem in developing the consensus necessary to make the direct election of the president effective.

The solution fixed on to solve this problem was the electoral college. Each state would put forward its leaders as its electors, and the college of these electors, made up of people with a broader national vision, would elect the president.

Again, as it turned out, this was also a solution to a problem that never developed. Right from the get-go, the political parties decided who the presidential candidates were going to be. When a state decided which candidate it was going to support, it would then just put together a slate of electors committed to voting for the candidate selected. But regardless, representative government was further compromised.

In addition to these structural deficiencies in representative government, our present form of campaign financing also works counter to representative government. Politicians are dependent on large donations to finance their campaigns (L 23,47,58,254).

There's no implication of bribery here. There's no quid pro quo – you do such and such and I'll contribute so much to your campaign.

Instead, donors, such as the energy industry and Wall Street, who are in a position to make large donations, support politicians who subscribe to positions that reflect those of the donors. As a consequence, we get no meaningful action on such things as climate control and financial industry regulation.

The alternative to our current system of funding campaigns is for the government to fund them. Such a program would have the following characteristics.

1. To reduce the expense of campaigning, the campaign period would be limited to some short time, such as seven weeks.
2. Candidates would be provided by the government with a fixed amount of campaign funds, which they can use in any way that they see fit.
3. Private contributions to campaigns would be prohibited.

At present, public funding of political campaigns is a dead letter. It has been tried.

The Federal Election Campaign Act of 1971 provided for public financing of presidential campaigns. The purpose of the act was to substitute public financing for private financing, and in conformance with this purpose, the act also limited private campaign expenditures.

In *Buckley v. Valeo* (1976), the Supreme Court, observing that making campaign contributions was a form of speech, struck down the act on the basis of the argument that limiting private campaign expenditures was an unconstitutional infringement of free speech. This argument is faulty, and the ruling should be reversed.

Bribery is a form of speech, but it's illegal, because it distorts representative government. Private funding of campaigns also distorts representative government, and consequently, should also be prohibited. (L 60)

To get rid of the electoral college and the Senate, constitutional amendments are required. If it proves to be impossible to reverse *Buckley v. Valeo*, then to institute publicly funded campaigns, a constitutional amendment is also required. Getting constitutional amendments adopted is going to require that a lot of politicians get on board.

One way to encourage politicians to act is by means of a grassroots movement with a dedicated leadership with enough power to force the government to adopt changes that would, otherwise, have been impossible (S 300). The black leadership, epitomized by Martin Luther King, and their movement to get civil rights legislation passed is an example.

Politicians will vote in favor of reform if people make it a single issue: Either you support reform or we won't vote for you, no matter what position you take on all of the other issues. The number of people with an interest in representative government outweighs the number that special interests can muster.

Deep pockets also influence politicians by offering them lucrative positions and contracts once they retire. All government officials should be prohibited, for at least five years, from accepting any form of employment from any for-profit organization (or any related trade organization, lobbying firm, etc.) that they regulated while in government. (R 191,192)

Another restraint on representative government is voting on Tuesday, because, on Tuesday, many people have to work (L 27). Early voting would solve this problem.

Gerrymandering (L 28) creates safe congressional districts. If it's a Republican safe district, then the Republican candidate is guaranteed victory. The Democratic candidate doesn't stand a chance. The equivalent situation is true for the Democratic candidate in a Democratic safe district.

As a result, in a safe district, incumbents don't have to worry about winning the election. It's in the primary where they face a challenge.

In a primary, the general public doesn't bother to vote. It's the ideologically committed, the extremists, who turn out to vote. So during their incumbency, the incumbents have to toe the party line and not fraternize with the opposing party for fear that, if they do, when the next primary comes along, they'll lose the nomination to someone who's more ideologically pure. (F 251,333)

The way to get rid of gerrymandering is to require that congressional districts be set up on a one-person/one-vote basis and that the contours of each district be as regular and compact as possible. There are computer programs that can carry out such a mandate. (D 246)

Sources

(D) De Mesquita, Bruce Bueno and Smith, Alastar *The Spoils of War* (Hachette 2016)

(F) Friedman, Thomas L. and Mandelbaum, Michael *That Used to Be Us* (Straus and Giroux 2011)

(L) Lessig, Lawrence *Republic, Lost* (Hachette 2015)

(R) Reich, Robert B. *Saving Capitalism* (Penguin Random House 2015)

(S) Stiglitz, Joseph E. *The Price of Liberty* (Norton 2012)

CHAPTER SEVENTEEN
Personal Money Management

Becoming a millionaire is, no longer, a big deal. However, it's still nothing to be sneezed at. And anyone with a steady job at a decent rate of pay can do it. It's not rocket science. There are just four things that you have to do.

Avoid debt
Be frugal
Save
Invest

AVOIDING DEBT

If you can borrow at one rate and invest in a sure thing at a higher rate, then go for it – borrow as much as you can. But such situations are rare to nonexistent. The opposite is the usual case. For example, a bank will charge you more to use its money than it will pay you for it to use yours.

Debt is dangerous. If you borrow money, you have to pay it back. When the time to pay back comes, you may find yourself in the situation where, to get the money to pay, you have to sell investments at a loss. That's not good. The fallback rule is: Don't borrow.

Leveraging

Ultimately, we're going to recommend that you invest in the stock market. Historically, over the long-term, the market returns ten percent.

Money is frequently available for less than ten percent. This suggests the idea of borrowing money with which to invest. This is leveraging your money, which can be remunerative. However, if those investments go down instead of up, you may have to sell those depreciated investments at what could be a devastating loss to pay back your debt.

Don't leverage.

Financing

Given that, over the long-term, the stock market returns ten percent, as a first cut, we could say that, if you can finance a purchase for less than ten percent, then you should finance and use the money made available by the financing to buy stock. But a qualification is necessary.

The market returns ten percent *over the long-term*. Other than a house, the things that you can finance, such as cars, furniture and appliances, have a financing period of two or three years. That's not long-term.

The market is volatile. Over the short-term, such as two or three years, the value of stocks can drop dramatically. You then pay all of that interest to free up money to buy stock that doesn't do anything but go down. So you have to be careful about financing. The general rule is: Don't finance – pay cash.

Unlike the value of things such as cars, furniture and appliances, which erodes, rather rapidly, with passing time, the age of a maintained house doesn't have much, if any, negative effect on its value. Over time, it typically increases in value. A house isn't just a residence. It has some of the aspects of an investment.

On the other hand, buying a house ties up a lot of your funds. And real estate isn't a recommended investment. It's illiquid, undiversified and leveraged.

So, if you don't have children or are an empty nester, rent, don't buy, and use the freed funds for investment. If you have children, then you're going to need substantial housing for a long while. Buying may then be the better bet.

Unlike financing things such as cars, furniture and appliances, mortgages can be taken out for 30 years, which is long-term. And historically, the mortgage rate has been less than ten percent.

So, if you decide that buying is your preferred option, take out the largest mortgage available. Not only does this free up cash for investing, you also get to take advantage of the mortgage interest deduction on your income tax.

Other than having a mortgage on a house in which you're raising children, you should avoid financing. Those interest payments are an impediment to accumulating savings.

Buying a car is a substantial outlay. Nevertheless, you shouldn't finance the purchase. Instead, you should pay cash.

You don't have the cash, but you still need a car? OK. Suppose that you finance the purchase of the car for three years.

Pay off the loan as soon as possible. Then, for each month of the next three years, deposit the payment that you'd have otherwise paid on your loan. At the end of the three years, you'll have saved enough money to buy your next car for cash. And while you're saving, you're earning interest on the money that you've saved. That's the situation that you want. You want other people to pay you interest for using your money rather than paying interest to other people for using their money.

BEING FRUGAL

Avoid unnecessary expenses.

Don't replace things until they wear out.

Don't buy such things as candy bars, bags of nuts, soft drinks, lottery tickets, bottled water, drinks at a bar, and other such stuff. You can do without them.

Don't buy a new car. Buy a used one. And drive it until it falls apart. It should last for, at least, 200,000 miles.

Don't subscribe to an Internet service. You can use the Internet at the library.

Don't buy a smartphone. A flip phone will give you all of the phone service that you need at a fraction of the cost. And, once you have a cell phone, you don't need a land line.

Don't buy newspapers and magazines. You can read them at the library.

Don't buy books or DVDs. You can borrow them from the library.

You don't need to buy lunch. You can brown bag it.

You don't have to wash your car. Just leave it out when it rains, and Mother Nature will wash it for you.

If where you're going is within a half-mile or so, don't drive. Walking or riding a bike is good for you.

If you don't have children or are an empty nester, rent, don't buy. Apartments come in a wide range of rents. Apartments at the low end of this range are adequate and comfortable. They're in mixed neighborhoods, but your neighbors will be friendly and unobtrusive. These apartments are in houses that are 100 years or more old that have been converted into two or three apartments. Your landlord may own two or three other houses in addition to the one in which you're living. He may live in one of his apartments. He'll be responsible and responsive.

When you experience a windfall, such as receiving a bonus or coming into an inheritance, you'll be inclined to celebrate, and a good way to celebrate is to spend the money. Resist the temptation. Put the money into your savings.

In sum, as Ben Franklin said, "Take care of the cents, and the dollars will take care of themselves."

SAVING

If your employer offers a defined contribution retirement plan (401(k)), participate to the maximum that the plan allows. If not, set up an IRA.

Be disciplined about saving. Fix on a specific amount that you're going to save each pay period. Then treat that amount the same way that you treat a utility bill. Each time that it comes due, which is every payday, pay the "savings bill" before spending your pay on other things.

There are people who don't earn enough to make ends meet, let alone save. And there are others who suffer some kind of catastrophe, such as a large medical bill or job loss, which wipes out their savings and then some.

It's argued that exhorting such people to save is, not only pointless, but also insulting. I agree.

Such people are candidates for welfare. But that doesn't relieve the bulk of us of the responsibility to save for the purpose of meeting large expenses that we can anticipate in the future, such as buying a house, educating our children, and providing for our retirement.

INVESTING

Once you've accumulated some money, you're ready to invest. The first thing that you have to do is understand the concept of liquidity.

Liquidity

Liquidity is the availability of counterparties. That is, when you want to sell something, there's someone who wants to buy. And when you want to buy something, there's someone who wants to sell.

Without liquidity, trading (the buying and selling of assets) is impossible. Yet we have no workable definition of liquidity, and we don't know enough about it to be able to quantify it.

There's an old Wall Street saying that liquidity is always there except when you need it. Mervyn King says, "Liquidity is an illusion; here one day, gone the next." (K 253)

Liquidity has to do with the ease with which you can, on short notice, convert an asset of yours into money without significantly affecting the price at which it's selling. For example, in normal circumstances, if you own a stock, you can call up your broker and he'll tell you the price at which your stock is selling, and if you decide to sell, the sale will go through right away, and you'll get close to the quoted price for your stock. What you get for your stock may be a little more or a little less than the quoted price, but it will be close. Your stock is a liquid asset.

(The qualification, "in normal circumstances", is necessary, because if the stock market goes into panic, which it sometimes does, most notably on October 19, 1987, when it fell 22.61 percent in a matter of minutes, the price of your stock may drop significantly between the time that you get the quote and the time that you sell, no matter how short that time interval is.)

If you own a house, it has what's known as a market value. That is, you can have an appraiser come in, and he'll tell you what the going price for your house is.

The appraiser may be off a little. (They generally prefer to err on the high side.) But they'll be pretty close to the mark, and if you wait long enough in a stable market, you'll probably be able to sell your house at or near its appraised value.

But that's the hooker. You can get the market price for your house, but you may not get it right away. Your house is an illiquid asset.

The liquidity of an asset has nothing to do with whether you'll be able to realize a profit when you sell your asset. The instant that you buy a stock, its price may begin to fall and continue to fall for as long as you hold onto the stock. It's a loser.

But the stock is still a liquid asset. At any time that you decide to dump it, you can call up your broker, he'll tell you what your dog is selling for, and when you sell, you'll get close to the price quoted.

Profitability and liquidity are different things. Profitability has to do with whether you can sell your asset for more than you bought it for. Liquidity has to do with whether you can sell your asset quickly at the quoted price.

Chances are that you're always going to be in the position where an occasion can arise where you're going to need to sell investments to raise cash on short notice. So you want to invest in liquid assets.

Investment Types

There are three main types of investments: *real estate* (residential and commercial), *collectibles* (such as antiques, coins, jewelry, art work, baseball cards, and comic books), and *securities*. Real estate and collectibles are illiquid.

The only liquid investment is securities. So, you want to invest in securities.

Securities

There are three types of securities: *stocks*, *bonds* and *derivatives*.

Derivatives

A derivative is a security that derives its value from the value of something else. The most common types of derivatives are options and futures.

An option is the right to either buy or sell some specified asset, known as the underlying asset, on or before some specified future date, known as the expiration date, at some specified price, known as the contract price, but entails no obligation to do so. Suppose that you buy an option to buy a specified amount of cocoa. When the market price of cocoa becomes more than the contract price, your option acquires value, because you can exercise the option, buy the specified amount of cocoa at the lower contract price, and sell it at the higher market price. The value of your option derives from the value of the underlying asset, which is why options are called derivatives.

But you don't have to exercise your option to realize its value. Since it has value, investors will be willing to pay you more for it than you paid to buy it. Selling options that they've previously purchased and that have acquired value is how option investors make money.

However, if by the expiration date, the price of cocoa has remained below the contract price, then your option will expire without ever having obtained any value, and you'll lose the money that you paid for it. That can hurt, and options buyers have been known to be burned badly.

A future is a contract that gives you both the right and the obligation to either buy or sell some specified asset at some specified price at some specified future date. Suppose that you buy a future to buy a specified amount of cocoa. If during the life of your future, the market price of cocoa becomes more than the contract price, your future will acquire value, because it's anticipated that, when the future matures, the market price will remain above the contract price, and you'll be able to buy the specified amount of cocoa at the contract price, sell it at the market price, and make a profit. The value of your future derives from the value of the underlying asset, which is why futures are called derivatives.

Because your future has value, investors will be willing to buy it from you for more than you paid for it. Selling futures that they've previously purchased and that have acquired value is how futures investors make money.

However, if when the future matures, the price of cocoa has remained below the contract price, then you're obligated to buy the cocoa at the contract price, even though the market price is less than the contract price. Actually, you don't have to carry out this obligation. What you do instead is buy an opposite future that cancels out your original future. But in addition to what you paid for the first future, that second future is also going to cost you, and the total cost can be severe. Under such circumstances, futures buyers have been known to be burned badly.

All derivatives (futures, options, and all of their more complex relatives, such as collateralized mortgage obligations) come with the potential for devastating losses. This isn't where you want to invest your savings. As my ol' Daddy used to say, "Don't gamble unless you can afford to lose."

Stocks and Bonds

Both stocks and bonds are viable investment vehicles. Which is more desirable is a question of what your investment horizon is.

If you're going to need a specific amount of money at a specific future date, this requirement sets a specific, short-term investment horizon for you. But in the absence of any such short-term horizons, your investment horizon is long-term.

When you're planning to buy a house, or when you want to finance your children's college education, you have a short-term investment horizon. But your general investment goal is long-term.

Over the long term, stocks return about twice as much as bonds. So if you can stand the market's volatility, the place to put your long-term investments is in stocks.

Volatility

Stocks are *volatile*. Before you invest in them, you have to be sure that you can handle this volatility, where you can see your savings shrink by as much as one half, maybe more.

For example, on March 23, 2000, the market topped out. The market then tanked, and when it had bottomed out on October 9, 2002, it had lost 50 percent of its value. That means that, if on March 23, 2000, you had $500,000 invested in the market, by October 9, 2002, you would have lost $250,000, a quarter of million dollars.

On October 9, 2007, the market, once more, topped out. By the time that the market reached its bottom on March 9, 2009, it had lost 56.6 percent of its value.

The stock market is volatile, but if you can take the sickening dips in the value of your investments as the market gyrates through its roller coaster ride, the market can be your friend.

When the market takes a dive, it's hard to just watch your money melt away. But you can't panic and sell. You've got to grit your teeth and hang tough, in the sure faith that, no matter how far the market falls, it will eventually recover and go on to achieve ever greater highs.

If you can't do this, you should stay out of the stock market, because you're going to find yourself selling low, which shrinks the value of your investments. Instead, you should invest in the lower yielding but more stable bond market.

Investing in Stocks

The stock market is volatile. One day, stocks are up. The next day, they're down. However, since you're investing for the long term, these day-to-day fluctuations are of no concern to you.

What you want to avoid is an investment that goes down and then stays down, which can happen to any stock.

But that isn't true of the stock market as a whole. No matter how far it drops, the market always recovers.

(All right. I agree. I can't logically rule out the possibility that the market may go down and stay down for good. But I'll say that, if such a thing were to occur, there wouldn't be much left of the world, so it probably wouldn't matter where you stashed your money, which likely wouldn't be worth much anyhow.)

So your strategy should be to not invest in individual stocks but to, instead, invest in the market as a whole. And that's possible. You invest in a broad-based *index fund*.

Managing Your Investments

The market is *cyclical*. First, it goes up. Then it goes down, only to subsequently, once more, go up.

In addition to being cyclical, the market has an underlying upward trend. Having your money in an index fund allows you to take advantage of this underlying trend.

But you can do better than that. You can also benefit from the market's cyclical nature.

When the market is making new highs, you should, from time to time, take money out of your index fund. And when the market is dropping, you should be putting money into your index fund. In this way, you're buying low and selling high, which is the way to make money.

You shouldn't trust your judgment, which is fallible, to make these investment moves. You should use a mechanical technique – choose a percentage. For example, suppose that you choose ten percent.

At some point, the market will make an all-time high and will then drop by more than ten percent. This all-time high then becomes the base on which you make your investment decisions.

Subsequently, the market will reach bottom and begin to turn around. Eventually, it will exceed its previous all-time high by ten percent. This is a signal for you to move some amount of money, X, out of your index fund.

The market may then go on to exceed its previous all-time high by 20 percent. This is a signal to move 2X amount of money out of your index fund. If the market then continues on and exceeds its previous all-time high by 30 percent, it's time to move 3X out of your index fund.

And so on. In following this investment strategy, you're emulating Baron Rothschild, who, when asked how he made his money, said that he made it by selling too soon.

When you move money out of your index fund, you're going to put it in either a savings account or a *money market account* (MMA). MMAs return more than savings accounts.

However, savings accounts are insured by the government and MMAs aren't, which means that MMAs carry some risk of losing value. But this risk is minimal. There's so much money tied up in MMA accounts, which people and organizations use to pay bills, that if MMA accounts get into trouble, the government will provide whatever support is necessary to prevent them from defaulting, as it did on September 19, 2008.

So the place to put your cash is in a MMA.

Eventually, the market will reach a new all-time high and then began to go down. If it falls ten percent below this new all-time high, the new all-time high becomes your new investment base.

At the same time, at this ten percent breakpoint, you should move X amount of money from your MMA back into your index fund. If the market falls 20 percent below your new base, you should then move 2X from your MMA into your index fund. If it falls 30 percent below your base, you should then move 3X from your MMA into your index fund. And so on, until the market bottoms out and begins to recover.

In pursuing this strategy, you're, once more, following Baron Rothschild's advice. He said, "The time to buy is when there's blood in the streets."

In other words, the time to buy is when things are bad. And the worse things get, the more that you should buy.

The cycle then repeats.

That's it: That's how you manage your investments. Buy low, sell high. It's not rocket science.

The ten percent interval between investment breakpoints is an arbitrary choice. You can adjust it as you will.

If you're more adventurous, you can shrink the interval. For example, you could set the breakpoints to occur at every five percent change.

If you're more cautious, you can expand the interval. For example, you could set the breakpoints to occur at every 20 percent change.

The wealthier that you are, the more you'll have in your index fund and the greater X, the unit of measure for the funds you move between your index fund and your MMA, should be.

There are just two qualifications. First, the market can really go crazy and enter an extended boom.

When that happens, you don't want to have previously pulled so much money out of your index fund that you've exhausted it and aren't in a position to benefit from the continuing boom.

So you want to set a limit below which you don't let the amount in your index fund drop. At some point, this limit will put a cap on the amount that you can move at any given positive breakpoint.

Where you set this limit is, again, a function of your wealth. The wealthier that you are, the higher the limit can be.

There's also a limit below which you shouldn't let the amount in your MMA drop. How to set this limit is a subject that we'll take up below, primarily when we discuss planning for retirement.

Complicating this investment program is the fact that there may be times when you have to draw funds out of your savings, and you have to prepare for these events. There are, at least, four such events — emergencies, buying a house, paying for your children's college education, and retiring. What you want to do is handle these events without having to draw money out of your index fund when the market is down, because that would mean selling low, which isn't the way to grow your investment fund.

Emergencies

When you need money to cover emergency expenses and the market is making new highs, there's no problem. You just take the money out of your index fund.

But when you need money to cover emergency expenses and the market is down, what you need is a cushion of money on which you can fall back rather than tap your index fund, a cushion that you keep in your MMA. The question is: How much should you stash away in your MMA for emergencies?

You don't want any more emergency money in your MMA than you need, because MMAs are notorious for not paying much of a return. On the other hand, you want enough to cover the cost of an emergency.

So, how much should you be setting aside for an emergency? I can't tell you. It has to be up to you. The more risk averse you are, the more emergency money you should have in your MMA.

The defining characteristic of an emergency is that you don't know when one will occur. That's why you need a cushion to fall back on.

Unlike emergencies, buying a house, paying for your children's college education, and retiring are things that can be anticipated and, therefore, planned for.

Buying a House

If you've decided to buy a house, you're going to need to come up with the down payment. If the stock market is making new highs, there's no problem. You just take the down payment out of your index fund.

But if the market is down, taking the down payment out of your index fund is what you don't want to do. So, some time before the house search gets serious, you want to have the down payment stashed away in your MMA, just in case that, when it comes time to make the down payment, the market is down. And of course, you want to stash the down payment away in your MMA when the market is making new highs.

Suppose that the market is now making new highs. Do you want to stash away the down payment at this time? Or do you want to wait a while?

After all, the market might continue to go up for some time yet, and if you wait, you can take full advantage of that bull market before you have to set aside the funds for the down payment. But suppose you wait and, instead of continuing to go up, the market turns around and goes down. Then what do you do?

So, what's the answer? Once more, I can't give you any advice. You're just going to have to make up your own mind in terms of your penchant for risk. If you're comfortable with risk, you might wait a while. If risk drives you crazy, you're better off setting aside the money now, getting it over with, and having some peace of mind.

Paying for Your Children's College Education

If you have children, you have to plan for their college education. Here you want an investment that will pay off exactly when you need the money. For example, suppose that you have one child who's going to start college in six years and you anticipate that this college education is going to cost $40,000 a year.

Assuming that you're not going to pay for this education out of pocket, then what you want is a $40,000 investment that's going to pay off in six years when your child begins college, a second investment of $40,000 that's going to pay off in seven years, a third investment that's going to pay off in eight years, and a fourth that's going to pay off in nine years. The type of investment that fills this bill is bonds.

The type of bond that you want is one that isn't going to default — that is, not pay off when it comes due. The bond least likely to default is a Treasury bond. So that's the bond that you should buy.

In the example above, what you want is $40,000 worth of Treasury bonds that are going to mature in six years, a second set of $40,000 worth of bonds that's going to mature in seven years, a third set that's going to mature in eight years, and a fourth set with a maturity date nine years from now. If you're going to meet some of the college expense for your child out of pocket, then you should adjust down the amount of bonds that you need accordingly.

You're going to pay for these bonds with money that you draw out of your index fund, and you want to make this withdrawal when the market is making new highs. So, you now face the same question that you did when it was time to set aside a down payment for buying a house.

For example, suppose that, currently, the market is making new highs. Should you buy the bonds now, or should you wait another year, so that your money can earn more before you take it out to buy the bonds?

Waiting another year is a good idea … if the market stays up. But if the market goes down, then you've got a narrow window of five years before you're going to need $40,000 to pay for the first year of your child's college education. If the market is still down when that time comes, you're going to have to take this money out of your index fund, and your investments are going to take a hit.

So, what's the answer? Once more, I can't give you any advice. You're just going to have to make up your own mind in terms of your penchant for risk.

Planning for Retirement

If when you retire, you have an adequate pension income, then there's no problem. You just meet your expenses with your pension income and continue the investment program that you were practicing before you retired.

But if, like many of us, your pension isn't adequate, then you're going to have to regularly withdraw funds from your investments to maintain your life style. At that point, you want to have enough of a money cushion in your MMA so that you can withdraw your maintenance cash from your MMA during any period when the market is down. Once more, the amount that you should set aside for this purpose is something that only you can decide.

First, you have to figure out how much you're going to need each year to support yourself. That shouldn't be too difficult.

But second, you also have to decide how long that you think that a market downturn can last. That's more difficult.

Beginning in 1929, the stock market went into a swoon, from which it didn't recover until 1952, 24 years later. If sometime during those 24 years, you were forced to sell stock to meet your needs, you'd experience a large, possibly devastating, loss.

However, the Great Depression may have been an anomaly. Since 1970, the stock market has experienced a number of recessions, but none of them have come close to the length of the Great Depression. The market went eight years, from 1973 to 1980, before it recovered the losses incurred in the interim. It went into another eight-year slump from 2000 to 2007. From 2009 until 2013, it was in a five year down period.

Your estimate of how long the market can stay down is going to depend on your tolerance for risk. The less that you can live with risk, the longer the period on which you should count.

Once you've made these two decisions, you multiply the amount that you need each year by the number of years of a down market that you think will be a maximum, and the product is how much you should have in your MMA in addition to your emergency funds.

But you still have one more decision to make. When you retire, you want that cash cushion to be sitting in your MMA. So, you're going to have to build it up in the years before you retire, and the question is: When do you start building it up?

This is analogous to the question of when you should set aside funds for a down payment on a house and when you should start buying those bonds to provide for your child's college education. You want to do it when the market is making new highs.

So, sometime before you retire, say ten years (the number that you actually use is one that you have to choose to suit your tolerance for risk), you should start thinking about moving money from your index fund into your MMA. You want to do this when the market is making new highs.

The market could be making new highs right at the start of the ten years. If not, your plan is that this will happen before you have to retire.

Once the market is making new highs, you then have to decide how long you're willing to wait before transferring money from your index fund to your MMA. The longer you wait, the more the amount in your index fund is going to grow ... provided that the market continues to make new highs.

But if you wait, and instead of continuing to make new highs, the market goes down, then you've got a problem. Once more, you have to make this decision on when to start building up the fund in your MMA for retirement on the basis of what makes you feel comfortable.

Managing Your Retirement

When the market is down, you should rely on your MMA to provide your retirement maintenance expenses. That will start to deplete the amount in your MMA.

But, no problem. When the market is, once more, making new highs, you'll be shifting funds from your index fund to your MMA, which will replenish the cushion in your MMA.

Final Considerations

The investment program described here will experience a significant, positive return as long as the money invested in index funds is a minority of the money invested in the stock market. To see why, think about the situation where everyone is following the investment program described here.

When the market is making new highs, everyone is going to want to move money from their index fund to their MMA (everyone is going to want to sell and no one is going to want to buy). And when the market is making new lows, everyone is going to want to move money from their MMA to their index fund (everyone is going to want to buy and no one is going to want to sell). The result would be financial chaos.

But not to worry. The possibility of such a development is remote.

Despite all of the evidence to the contrary, people are going to continue to believe that they can beat the market and are going to eschew investing in index funds in favor of an active investment strategy. And people are going to continue to panic and sell when the market makes a dramatic drop. As has been truly said, the stock market is the only market where people run for the exit when a sale is going on but beat down the doors to get in when prices are going up. Until we abolish greed and fear, index fund investing will remain viable and profitable.

Sources

(K) King, Mervyn *The End of Alchemy* (W. W. Norton 2016)

INDEX

Printed in the United States
by Baker & Taylor Publisher Services